THE ECONOMICS OF PASTORALISM

THE ECONOMICS OF PASTORALISM

A Case Study of Sub-Saharan Africa

Z. A. Konczacki

FRANK CASS

First published 1978 in Great Britain by
FRANK CASS AND COMPANY LIMITED
Gainsborough House, Gainsborough Road,
London E11 1RS, England

and in the United States of America by
FRANK CASS AND COMPANY LIMITED
c/o Biblio Distribution Centre,
81 Adams Drive, P.O. Box 327, Totowa, N. J. 07511

British Library Cataloguing in Publication Data

Konczacki, Z A
    The economics of pastoralism.
    1. Stock and stock-breeding — Economic aspects —
    Africa, Sub-Saharan
    I. Title
    338.1'7'600967   SF55.A3

    ISBN 0-7146-3086-1

Typeset by Computacomp (UK) Limited
*Printed in Great Britain by offset lithography by
Billing & Sons Limited, Guildford, London and Worcester*

To the memory of my Parents

CONTENTS

PREFACE

My interest in the pastoral economies of Africa dates back to the 1960s, when I had an opportunity to travel to Botswana and Somalia to acquaint myself with the problems of those countries. When I went to Somalia as an economic adviser, I came in contact with the phenomenon of pastoral nomadism and it was there that my ideas first began to germinate. Events and developments of subsequent years still further stimulated my interest, contributing to the evolution and the final formulation of my thoughts on pastoralism.

The consequences of the disastrous droughts in Africa of the early 1970s confirmed my suspicions that the policies of the governments of the countries most affected by the environmental catastrophe were inadequate or even outright inappropriate. These events influenced me to write a book on the economics of pastoralism in the hope that the analysis contained in it, and the suggestions and proposals put forward, will assist these countries in a search for a solution to the pastoral dilemma in Africa.

During the course of my research I was disappointed by the indifference on the part of professional economists towards the problem of pastoralism. This fact still further stimulated my determination to come to grips with the problem.

Most of the literature on pastoralism falls within the area of anthropology, natural sciences, and environmental studies. Anthropologists must be credited with the accumulation of a large amount of extremely valuable material of a qualitative rather than quantitative nature. They have made an outstanding contribution by identifying and describing the traditional pastoral attitudes and sets of values which form their basis. Natural scientists and agronomists concentrated their studies of pastoralism mainly on the question of livestock raising and range management. On the other hand, the harsh and precarious ecological conditions of the pastoral areas has attracted the attention of environmentally-minded scientists. The contribution of environmentalists, however, lies primarily in their emphasis on global interdependence in the area of natural resources and the dangers involved in human interventions in the ecosystems which disregard a 'holistic' approach. Being of the opinion that these aspects cannot be overemphasized, an economic dimension is added in this work by the author.

The mode of presentation takes into account not only the policy-makers in the African countries but also the interests of a wide range of students of social and natural sciences. The differences in the tools of analysis and terminology between their disciplines and economics should not present a barrier. For this reason, the use of economic models is limited to a necessary minimum and the number of variables is restricted to those which are considered the most crucial. The approach is far more policy-oriented than theoretical. Theory only proves its value when it can serve as a basis for formulating a framework for reform of the pastoral sector.

Extensive use has been made of some of the results of my explorations in the field of the economic history of pastoral communities. The findings serve as an indispensable background for the understanding of the past and the present. Areas where further research is needed have come to light. The need for data collection on a scale far exceeding the material resources of the present writer has been indicated.

The realization of this project would not have been possible without the assistance of all those who provided me with the necessary sources of information and data. I should like to thank especially Mr. Abdurahman Hussein, Chargé d'Affaires, Somali Embassy, Washington, D.C., Mr. M. Modisi, First Secretary of the Embassy of Botswana, Washington, D.C., Dr. Hugh O. H. Vernon-Jackson, First Secretary (Development) of the Canadian

High Commission in Nigeria, Dr. J. H. Hollomon, Director of the Center for Policy Alternatives, Massachusetts Institute of Technology, Dr. Keith Bezanson, Chief Project Officer, Commonwealth Division of the Canadian International Development Agency, Ottawa, L. G. Grimble and Associates Limited, Project Planning Associates Limited, and Enelco Limited of Canada, Dr. Edward F. Szczepanik, Food and Agriculture Organization, Rome, Mr. W. Sikorski, The World Bank, Washington, D.C., and Dr. T. M. Shaw, Director of the African Studies Centre, Dalhousie University, Halifax, N.S., Canada.

I wish to express my appreciation to the staffs of the Public Record Office, and the International African Institute in London, as well as the librarians of the Commonwealth Office Library, London, International Development Research Centre, Ottawa, and the Killam Memorial Library at Dalhousie University.

To my colleagues Professors P. B. Huber and U. L. G. Rao, who read parts of the manuscript and offered valuable comments, I owe a debt of gratitude. Needless to say none of the above persons or institutions is in any way responsible for any of the opinions I have expressed in this book.

I am also grateful to the Izaak Walton Killam Memorial Trust for financial help during the period of my Senior Research Fellowship in the Department of Economics, Dalhousie University, to the Canada Council which covered part of the cost of my research in England, and to Dalhousie University for granting me my sabbatical in 1975, which permitted me to conclude my research.

Special thanks are due to my wife whose unfailing encouragement helped me in completing this work.

Halifax, Nova Scotia   Zbigniew A. Konczacki
January 1978

Chapter One

INTRODUCTION

The main theme of this book is pastoralism and its economic aspects in sub-Saharan Africa. In terms of a wider approach some of the conclusions reached in this study may be applicable to other parts of the world, where similar conditions exist.

The drought that affected the Sahel in the early 1970s, and the large-scale hunger which struck millions of people, makes one aware of the possibility of such periodic disasters elsewhere. It also highlights the most tragic aspects of the world food crisis and exposes our inability to prevent such situations from arising in the absence of adequate planning. Rapid population growth and the vagaries of the climate are largely responsible for the precariousness of the global food situation and every opportunity of increasing the present food supply should be given serious consideration. Of particular value are the possibilities of adding to the supply of protein of animal origin without, at the same time, encroaching upon the lands suitable for the production of vegetable foods.

It is not a mere coincidence that in Africa the economic significance of pastoralism is greatest in many of those countries that have been identified as the least developed. Aridity or semi-aridity of the climate, characteristic of the large part of the area of those countries, constitutes the most serious barrier to the development of their economies. At the same time, it also determines the nature of economic activity for the majority of the people. The main source of livelihood is livestock raising and because of the nature of the environment it frequently assumes one of the several forms of pastoralism.

Pastoralism is an economic activity in which man and the herds of domesticated animals live in a symbiotic relationship. It is either carried on as the main form of subsistence, or it is combined with crop production.[1] But even if the population of an area is primarily engaged in pastoral activities the economy depends also on agricultural goods which it acquires by various means.[2]

Since pastoralism involves the maintenance of self-sustaining herds in pasture, cases when small numbers of livestock are raised by farmers on farm lands cannot be included under this term. Similarly, herds forming part of an artificially organized commercial enterprise have to be distinguished from the true communities of pastoralists for whom pastoralism is a way of life.[3]

There are a number of distinctions in the typology of the pastoral peoples. The basic distinction lies between pastoral nomadism in its pure form, semi-nomadism, and transhumance.[4] As a rule, pastoral nomads do not practise agriculture and they raise livestock for food consumption and exchange. They have no permanent place of abode and are involved in movements of a seasonal nature, often described as the pastoral nomadic cycle.[5]

Semi-nomads, on the other hand, are engaged in unspecialized herding-farming, i.e. a mixed form of subsistence. People practising this form of semi-pastoralism move back and forth from herding to farming; the latter occupation takes place in permanent settlements. However, no rigid and watertight classification is possible as there are always groups of pastoralists that cannot be strictly defined.

Finally, there is transhumance which is a more highly developed form of pastoralism than semi-nomadism. It is practised by sedentary people whose main economic activity is farming. Pastoral movements are seasonal and limited in scale involving a small proportion of the population, as livestock is taken care of by the cowherds, shepherds, or goatherds who specialize in their tasks.[6]

According to the old theory the stage of pastoral nomadism

generally precedes that of settled agriculture. In this evolutionary sequence nomads were compelled to clear land for cultivation when, due to population pressure, they could no longer subsist by raising livestock in natural grasslands.[7] More recent speculations on the origins of nomadism suggest a reversed sequence.[8] It is a matter of logic to presume that domestication of herd animals took place in sedentary societies. Hunters and nomads would not have been able to produce domestic generations out of captive animals.

However, the history of domestication is of limited relevance in the African context. The herding animals with which we are mainly concerned, such as cattle, camels, sheep and goats, were already domesticated before their arrival on the African continent.[9]

The sequence indicating a passage from settled farming to pastoral nomadism is confirmed by historical examples. A typical case in question is that of the Jie people of north-eastern Uganda who, some two hundred years ago, split into two groups. One group, under the old name − Jie − continued their existence as mixed farmers. Their economy consisted of millet farming and animal husbandry, the latter operated under a system of transhumance. The other group descended the Rift Valley escarpment into the Tarac Valley and became known under a new name − the Turkana. The secessionists changed to pastoral nomadism with practically no agriculture and with total dependence on their animals for subsistence.[10]

In many parts of Africa prolonged cultivation in relatively short rotations and frequent burning transformed forest and bush into savannah − a healthy grassland free of the tsetse fly and parasitic diseases creating thereby a favourable environment for the grazing of animals.[11]

In the chapters which follow our interest is directed towards the arid zones where the annual rainfall is below 500 millimetres.[12] It is there that large areas of grazing land are found. Because of deficient and erratic rainfall these lands are hardly suitable for the successful cultivation of unirrigated starch-food crops. Apart from the distribution of annual rainfall another vital climatic characteristic which must be taken into account, when determining the suitability of a given area for cultivation, is the

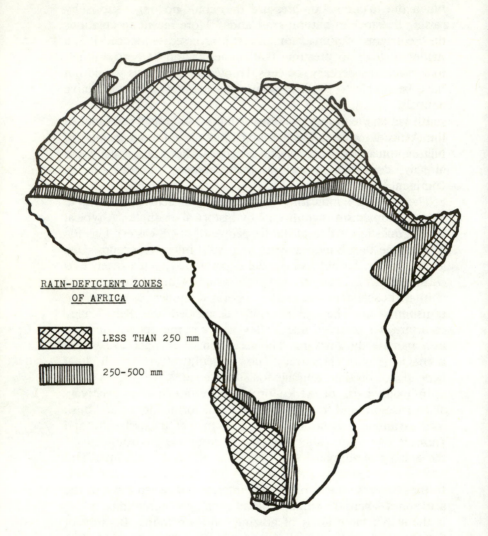

RAIN-DEFICIENT ZONES
OF AFRICA

LESS THAN 250 mm

250-500 mm

degree of evaporation during the growing season. It depends on the conditions of temperature, which change with the seasons of the year and the elevation above the sea level.

The ecological characteristics of the arid zones place a limitation on capital investment for pasture improvement. Adjustment of stock numbers to natural feed resources is the main problem which faces the pastoralist there.[13]

In sub-Saharan Africa grazing lands extending in the rain-deficient areas are found in the north and the east, as well as in the south-western parts of the continent. In the Sahel the southern limit runs from Dakar and then follows the northern frontier of Nigeria towards Lake Chad; then it runs to the east crossing the White Nile and turning in a north-easterly direction to join the Red Sea coast at Massawa. In the east of the continent the borderline follows the ridge of the Ethiopian mountains leaving Eritrea as well as a large part of Harrar, the whole of the Somali Democratic Republic and northern and eastern Kenya within the rain-deficient area. It eventually reaches Lake Rudolf and turns in a south-easterly direction excluding the Kenyan highlands and cutting into Tanzanian territory.

In the south-western part of Africa the northern boundary of the rain-deficient area begins south of Lobito in Angola and runs southwards, eventually turning east along the northern frontiers of Namibia and Botswana. Furthermore, it includes a belt of Rhodesian territory, approximately 160 kilometres wide, and having reached the border of Mozambique, it turns in a south-westerly direction cutting through the territories of Northern Transvaal, the Orange Free State, and Cape Province ending on the Atlantic coast somewhere north of Cape Town.[14]

As it has been previously pointed out aridity of the climate and serious developmental problems as a rule go together. It is for this reason that this book is primarily concerned with some of the least developed African economies.

In the framework of the international strategy for development during the Second U.N. Development Decade twenty-five countries have been designated as least developed. Of these sixteen are in Africa.[15] Later on, when the concept of the 'New International Economic Order' was adopted by the U.N. member nations, the old division into three worlds gave way to a new and more realistic fivefold grouping. The 'Fifth World' to which the least developed economies were relegated comprises countries that have problems of their own and special measures are needed to solve them. Pessimists may say that unlike other less developed countries these economies are destined to rely on foreign aid for an indefinite period of time.

In identifying the least developed economies in 1971, the Committee for Development Planning used four indicators: per capita gross domestic product (GDP), the rate of growth of GDP, the share of manufacturing in GDP, and the literacy rate in the age group fifteen years and over. The cut-off points were US$100 for per capita product, a share of manufacturing in GDP of less than 10 per cent, and a literacy ratio of less than 20 per cent for the relevant age group.

Questions were raised regarding the reliability of some of these indicators, claiming that these criteria were arbitrary. It has also been pointed out by the critics that GDP suffers as an indicator from its aggregative nature and imprecisions in its estimation.[16] In view of the criticisms some additional criteria were applied but even then these countries were in a worse position than the remaining less developed economies.[17]

Of the least developed economies of Africa six are typical arid zone countries. These are Botswana, Somalia, Sudan, Chad, Niger, and Mali. Among those economies only Botswana and Niger have recently developed mining activities of any significance. Agriculture in these countries is based mostly on pastoral production and farming takes a small proportion of both land and labour force.

In our group of countries harsh ecological conditions and consequently a very limited supporting capacity of land is reflected in an exceptionally low average number of persons per square kilometre. Population density ranges from one person per square kilometre in Botswana to seven persons in the Sudan, whereas the average for Africa as a whole is about 15 persons per square kilometre.[18]

The data on land use in these countries, scanty as they are, indicate how insignificant is the proportion of land under crops. In Botswana over 99 per cent, and in Niger nearly 88 per cent, of the total area of the country is taken by permanent meadows, pastures, forests and other areas excluding cultivated land. These are the highest and the lowest percentages recorded between 1960 and 1973.[19]

The importance of livestock in the economy accentuates the role played by pastoral activities. Comparisons between these economies based on animal units (A.U.) per capita of human populations bring out the relative significance of this factor. In terms of this criterion Botswana with 2.79, and Somalia with 2.14 A.U. per capita in 1974, appear to be well ahead of the remaining least developed countries situated in the arid zone, namely the Sudan with 0.90, Mali with 0.82, Niger with 0.75, and Chad with 0.73 A.U. per person. Among the least developed African economies outside the arid zone only Ethiopia with 0.90 A.U. per inhabitant approaches the level of the former group of countries. It is followed by Tanzania with 0.71 A.U. per inhabitant, while the remaining eight least developed economies remain far behind this level.[20]

These few indicators provide an initial approach to a discussion which follows in the ensuing chapters. Their main purpose is to bring out some of the features essential to our choice of the economies we shall concentrate on. Before a further justification of the choice of our case studies is provided and the plan of the book outlined, let us first adduce our grounds for assigning importance to pastoralism as a mode of production and the role it can play in economic development in the arid zone.

Large areas of the countries situated in the rain-deficient zone possess a developmental potential in so far as it is suited for grazing. It is either being misused due to the lack of a scientifically controlled approach to its exploitation, or it has been unutilized because of poor accessibility. In many cases these barriers can be removed with a modest investment in the necessary infrastructural arrangements. The opportunity cost of land and labour in these areas is practically nil, since the soil is not suited for any use other than grazing, and in the absence of alternative avenues of local employment of any significance, pastoralism remains the way most people earn their livelihood. On the other hand, the development and management of the pastoral sector would require a fraction of the capital investment needed for irrigated farming, provided conditions are present for its introduction on a scale sufficient to effect a complete change-over from pastoral nomadism to sedentary farming.

Sedentarization of pastoral nomads who, in terms of our typology, represent an extreme case, is not an unequivocal solution. As a rule, they strongly oppose such a change and submit to it only under duress. Socio-psychological traits alone cannot provide sufficient explanation of their resistance to change. Need for mobility may account for the 'wanderlust' instinct. But little is done through scientific research to investigate this psychological characteristic and its implications.[21] A contrast between free and leisurely nomadic existence and the toilsome life of a sedentary farmer may account for the scornful attitude of a nomad towards those who cultivate the soil. This feeling of superiority is based on a strong economic foundation: as long as the population of a pastoral region is sufficiently sparse, livelihood can be obtained with a minimal input of labour per unit of output. Given his mental attitude, conditioned by his isolation from the rest of the world and the material constraints imposed by the requirement of perpetual mobility, a nomadic pastoralist is deprived of strong stimuli to increase his productivity. Moreover, he hardly feels the need for cultural progress. These characteristics are deplored by his government which, as a rule, is committed to the idea of development.

In the past, many countries tried to solve this problem through resettlement schemes which aimed at a 'once and for all' sedentarization of the nomads. It is doubtful whether any good results were achieved through the indiscriminate implementation of such schemes. They led to the abandonment of pastures and the irretrievable loss of the traditional pastoral know-how. The change involved a trade-off between an increased output of the products of sedentary farming and the production of animal protein foods by pastoralists. The resources involved in the large-scale resettlement schemes could have been invested instead in the improvement of pastoral methods of production. It is this last point that deserves further consideration. First and foremost, the losses resulting from the unorganized exploitation of pasture-lands should be eliminated. The next step would be to take advantage of the largely unrealized potentialities. It is one of the contentions of this book that such a transformation is possible and that it can open a way to further and far-reaching improvements. The present pattern of land use results in the overexploitation of pastures and it precludes the application of rational methods of

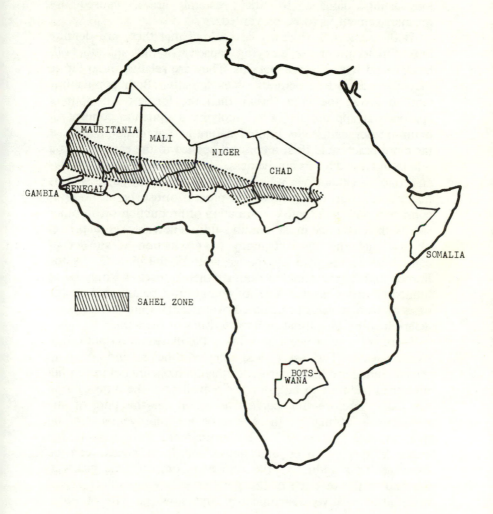

MAURITANIA

MALI

NIGER

CHAD

GAMBIA

SENEGAL

SOMALIA

SAHEL ZONE

BOTS-
WANA

range management. In many parts of Africa improvements in the institutional aspects of land use are imperative if irreparable or long-lasting damage to the pastoral areas, caused by mismanagement, is to be prevented.

At the same time it must be realized that there are definite limits, in terms of the carrying capacity of the land, to both human and livestock populations. They are relative in so far as they depend on the methods of exploitation. Both populations tend to grow, the latter faster than the former. An optimal approach is appropriate here, implying a dynamic concept of optimum population. Its limited nature and application make it far more practicable than a concept applied to the economy as a whole and noted for its elusiveness. The optimal approach implies an economic situation in which output produced by pastoralists is maximized. But the productive process must be at a level consistent with indefinite continuation of production or, in other words, the pasturage must remain a fully renewable resource. Let us also add that the efficiency of production is subject to constraints represented by the vagaries of the climate. As the introduction of measures to mitigate their impact can only be of limited effectiveness, the level of output must be assessed on the basis of average values calculated over a certain number of years determined by the climatic characteristics of the area.[22]

There are several ways of utilizing the increased output of the pastoral sector. The task of assigning priorities should be left to the individual producers, provided their choices are not in conflict with the system of social priorities prevailing at the time, and do not call, therefore, for corrective action on the part of the government. Primarily, there can be an improvement in the quantity and quality of local consumption. Furthermore, the available surplus, over and above the local needs, can be exported, thus adding to the money incomes of the pastoralists and to the revenue of the governments who collect export taxes. The relative insignificance and slow growth of intra-African trade is often related to the extremely limited range of goods which are of interest to prospective importers. Livestock and livestock products are a notable exception. Overseas exports are subject to the health regulations of the importing countries, and adequate processing of the products is of decisive importance.

The issues that have been mentioned here receive a theoretical treatment in the next two chapters, which provide a background for an empirical study of the selected sub-Saharan countries. Two models of pastoralism corresponding to the different stages of development state the conditions necessary for the maintenance of a long-term equilibrium situation and explain the reasons for the occurrence of deviations from these conditions. They also set the stage for the modern developmental effort aiming at increased productivity and preservation of the natural resource represented by the range. This theme is developed in a section dealing with the question of the scientific management of pastoral lands. Because in a pastoral economy livestock assumes the role of a capital asset, its nature and the problems of its accumulation are examined. Positive methods of finding a way out of the apparent impasse facing pastoral economies are contrasted with a negative approach represented by efforts to sedentarize the nomads.

The three chapters which follow are devoted to the case studies of Somalia, the economies of the Sahel, and Botswana. The first concentrates on the economic aspects of nomadic pastoralism, as approximately two-thirds of Somalia's population are nomads, and semi-nomadism is not insignificant in that country. A review of economic planning, going back to the 1950s, and of the factors which led to the dramatic growth of livestock exports, is followed by a discussion of the measures applied by the Government to deal with the ravages caused by the recent drought, and the problems which still remain to be solved.

The theme of natural disaster is continued in the next chapter and is illustrated with experiences from the Sahel. Particular attention is drawn to the errors in economic policies which permitted the occurrence of widespread hunger and enormous losses in animal population. Several proposals to reform the economies of the Sahel-Sudan belt are reported and the plausibility of their implementation is discussed in a critical vein.

In a separate chapter, dealing with Botswana, a study is made of a livestock sector, where pastoral activity assumes the form of transhumance. Botswana's meat and livestock exports are of considerable importance and only in the early 1970s did they drop to second place, a change which was due to major mineral discoveries. Of special interest is a recent proposal made by the government to solve the problem of common property rights to pastoral lands, thus opening the way for a scientifically controlled range management.

The concluding chapter reviews the alternative approaches to the solution of the question of pastoralism in sub-Saharan Africa.

In an attempt to arrive at a synthetic view of the matter, reference is made to the steady state model evolved earlier in this study, and it is indicated how its usefulness can be enhanced by adapting it to modern conditions. A proposal is made for far-reaching pastoral reform involving the introduction of an insurance scheme for pastoral nomads affording protection against natural calamities.

Taking a broader view, the supply of livestock products is considered in the light of the world food problem, and the viability of the present methods of meat production in the more developed countries is critically examined.

The final conclusions reveal the existence of resources capable of alternative uses, whose availability suggests a need for a revision of the commonly held views on the global food situation.

NOTES

1. L. Krader, 'Pastoralism'. *Encyclopaedia of Social Sciences*, 1968.
2. Economic history of Africa provides examples of a parasitic relationship practised by nomadic pastoralists, who exacted tribute from sedentary farmers or owned slaves who farmed for them in oases. But the complementarity of the outputs of the nomadic and the sedentary peoples and the resulting normal exchange of products between them cannot be overemphasized. For more information on this point see D. L. Johnson, *The Nature of Nomadism*. Chicago: The University of Chicago, Department of Geography Research Papers, 1969, 11–12
3. L. Krader, *loc. cit.*
4. The term pastoral nomads is used purposely in order to avoid confusion with other kinds of nomadism such as e.g. nomadic farmers (shifting cultivation), or nomadic hunters and gatherers.
5. D. L. Johnson, *loc. cit.*, 4–5.
6. L. Krader, *loc. cit.*
7. A new theory which suggests a reversed sequence implies that population pressure on agricultural resources had been mainly responsible for the development of pastoral nomadism in the ecological regions where settled farming was not possible.
8. E. Hahn, *Die Haustiere und ihre Beziehungen zur Wirtschaft des Mensches; eine Geographische Skizze.* Leipzig 1896. Hahn was the first to suggest that sedentary agriculturalists were responsible for the origins of both domestication and pastoral nomadism. Xavier de Planhol, 'Nomades

et Pasteurs I'. *Revue Géographique de l'Est*, vol. 1, no. 3, 1961; 291–310. J. F. Downs, *Domestication: an examination of the changing social relationships between man and animals*. Kroeber Anthropological Society Papers, no. 22, 1960; 18–67, cited in B. Spooner, *The Cultural Ecology of Pastoral Nomads*. An Addison-Wesley Module in Anthropology, no. 45, 1973; 5–6. The latter source provides a good summary of views on the beginnings of nomadism. See also C. O. Sauer, *Agricultural Origins and Dispersals*. Cambridge: The MIT Press, 1969, and E. Boserup, *The Conditions of Agricultural Growth*. Chicago: Aldine Publishing Company, 1965.

9. C. O. Sauer, *op. cit.*, 86. For a detailed discussion of the origins and stages of domestication see F. E. Zeuner, *A History of Domesticated Animals*. London: Hutchinson, 1963; chapter two. The possibility that apart from Arabia camels were also domesticated in Somalia is considered by R. W. Bulliet in his book *The Camel and the Wheel*. Cambridge, Mass: Harvard University Press, 1975.

10. P. H. Gulliver, *The Family Herds*. London: Routledge & Kegan Paul, 1955; 2–5.

11. E. Boserup, *op. cit.*, 20–21.

12. The problem of drawing a borderline between the rain-deficient and rain-sufficient regions of Africa has been dealt with on the basis of sparse or unreliable observations. M. K. Bennett, ('An Agroclimatic Mapping of Africa', *Food Research Institute Studies*, vol. 3, no. 3, 1962) uses the 250 mm isohyet for this purpose, whereas H. L. Shantz ('Agricultural Regions of Africa, Part 1 – Basic Factors', *Economic Geography*, January 1940) adopted the 500 mm isohyet. In terms of Bennett's criterion the rain-deficient area covers 14.55 million square kilometers, or 48.8 per cent of the total area of Africa. If this is compared to Shantz's estimate of 13.52 million square kilometers, or 45.0 per cent of the total, the difference does not appear significant. See also J. Phillips, *Agriculture and Ecology in Africa*. London: Faber and Faber, 1959.

13. W. Davies and C. L. Skidmore, 'Problems of Pasture Improvements' in *Tropical Pastures* ed. by W. Davies and C. L. Skidmore. London: Faber and Faber, 1966; 23.

14. Based on M. K. Bennett, *loc. cit.*

15. The following countries were included: Botswana, Burundi, Chad, Dahomey, Ethiopia, Guinea, Lesotho, Malawi, Mali, Niger, Rwanda, Somalia, Sudan, Tanzania, Uganda, and Upper Volta.

16. *U.N. Survey of Economic Conditions in Africa, 1972*, Part I. New York 1973; 280–281. In identifying the least developed countries the Committee did not always adhere to the originally stated cut-off points. Among countries included in the group the highest annual growth rate of GDP was 5.4 per cent (Guinea).

17. *Ibid*. The additional criteria used were: the value of agricultural output as a percentage of GDP; agricultural population as a percentage of labour force; export as a percentage of GDP; exports per capita; electricity consumption in Kwh per capita; and roads in kilometres per 1000 square kilometres.

18. The respective population densities are as follows: Botswana 1, Somalia 5, Sudan 7, Chad 3, Niger 3, Mali 5; based on 1974 population estimates. In the remaining African least developed countries population densities range between 14 in Burundi and 42 in Malawi.

19. Based on FAO, *Production Yearbook*, 1974, 3. 'Other areas' include potentially productive land, built-on-areas, etc., but the bulk of it can probably be classified as wasteland.

20. Animal units are calculated on the basis of conversion factors which are 1.1 for camels, 0.8 for cattle, and 0.1 for sheep and goats. *Ibid.*, 285. In spite of an element of arbitrariness present in a weighting system of this kind, there are no important reasons for questioning the validity of our comparisons.

21. H. V. Muhsam, 'Sedentarization of the Bedouin in Israel', *International Social Science Journal*, vol. 11, no. 4, 546.

22. The difficulties of this approach, particularly the problem of the periodicity of climatic changes, will be dealt with in the next chapter.

Chapter Two

A SOCIO-ECONOMIC FRAMEWORK OF PASTORALISM

Preamble

By way of introduction let us provide a concise description of the conditions and patterns of life in an environment to which the models developed in this chapter apply.

The two necessities of pastoral activity are pasturage and water. Their spatial distribution tends to be uneven and is largely influenced by seasonal changes in the weather. Hence, in an attempt to maximize the input of these two resources nomadic movements must be made. Moreover, the nature of pasturage and the distribution of watering points determine the composition of herds. Dietary needs differ between the various species of animals. At one extreme, cattle subsist mainly on grass and require frequent watering, thus being confined to grasslands over which watering points are adequately distributed. At the other extreme, camels need to browse and seldom to graze. Also, they have to be watered at much less frequent intervals than other herding animals. Sheep and goats live on both grass and leafage of trees as well as bushes. These factors are responsible for the way in which the herds are split into groups according to the type of animal. It may also be noted that the size of a group influences the frequency of its movements: the bigger the herd the more quickly will local supply of feed be exhausted.

The necessity of free movement is reflected in the form of ownership of land prevalent in the pastoral societies. Within the boundaries of a people's territory the range is a common property resource,[1] while livestock is privately owned by individuals or families.

Frequent and unhampered movement is the essence of the pastoral nomad's mode of life. As a result he owns few things and his possessions are carried on the backs of the beasts of burden. Hence the accumulation of wealth, other than livestock, becomes an encumbrance. As a consequence of this, his cultural development is restricted and his way of life remains largely unchanged. The relativity of values adopted by him is best expressed by stating that what sedentary societies would consider as deprivation is cherished by the nomad as freedom.

The availability of rangeland, together with the size of human population, impose limits within which livestock population can change. Variations consciously introduced by pastoralists are, as a rule, the expression of a conflict between the aims of economic efficiency on the one hand, and the viability of the system on the other. The first aim implies the maintenance of a herd of optimum size and structure relative to the range available and the consumption needs of the human population. The other goal, that of security, requires some measure of insurance against emergency situations. Its magnitude is usually based on vague empiricism and it often shows itself as a tendency to maximize animal population. The reasons for doing this are obvious enough: protection against famine, if drought occurs, and greater probability of survival of sufficient number of animals needed to recreate the depleted herd.

An 'idealized' model of a pastoral economy

A model of the pastoral economy can be expressed in terms of five variables of which two are exogenous and three endogenous to the system. Out of a large number of the variables identifiable in a pastoral economy only those of strategic importance have been selected for inclusion in the model. The decision to limit the number of variables to a minimum has been dictated by the approach which, at this stage of our analysis, is purely expository.

The variables reflect some of the realities of the pastoral world. Other realities, implicitly included in the model, are assumed here to remain unchanged over a long period of time.

These generally accepted realities, incorporated whether explicitly or implicitly in the model, are as follows:[2]

1. The range can tolerate a certain annual cropping rate beyond which rapid decline in the plants' regenerative powers occurs.
2. The range is a 'common property resource'. Its use is free within the limits of its availability.
3. The pastoral society consists of family units who maintain themselves chiefly by livestock-raising.
4. The set of priorities discernible in pastoral behaviour reflects the herders' desire to maximize their expected welfare.
5. Some of the pastoralists' social values, which have been formed under the impact of environmental pressures, are important determinants of their economic and fertility behaviour.
6. Apart from efforts to achieve dietary sufficiency pastoralists have no direct control over their own mortality.

Changes in the first exogenously determined variable – human population – depend on its fertility and mortality rates. Fertility behaviour has already been assumed to be largely dependent on the pastoralists' social values which for the purpose of our model are considered to be stable. Mortality depends on the natural conditions of pastoral life. Dietary sufficiency may become a critical factor influencing it during acute droughts. Both these influences can then be legitimately taken as being of exogenous nature.

Variations in the other exogenous variable, viz. the range, are outside the control of the pastoralists as they are unable to increase its total area by way of a conscious and direct effort. However, they can make decisions as to the degree of its utilization. It may be added that irregularities in rainfall lead to changes in the condition of the range and consequently in the availability of forage which can be considered as equivalent to a change in the area of rangeland of constant annual productivity.

Let us now consider the endogenous variables. The quantity of animals, given livestock fertility, which a pastoral society strives to maintain, depends on the size of the human population and on the availability of rangeland. It also depends on the rate of off-take as defined below.

The second endogenous variable of strategic importance is the off-take. It provides for the consumption requirements of the human population, which has been assumed to have no other means of support. The off-take consists of meat and milk, as well as of hides and skins. It is also convenient to include under the heading of off-take the losses of livestock due to natural causes.

The third endogenous variable is the cost of producing the off-take. It reflects the effort required of the pastoral population to satisfy its needs. Its upper limit is determined by the potential total amount of effort, which depends on the size of the labour force and the average amount of effort obtainable from its members. The actual demand for labour depends on the size of the animal population and the number of man-hours needed per animal, since each animal forming part of the total productive 'livestock-capital' necessitates some measure of attention.[3]

Let us now combine the five variables, enumerated above, into a model of a purely theoretical nature, whose purpose is to serve as a point of departure for an exercise which will eventually attempt to achieve a closer approximation to reality. The model is theoretical in the sense that it does not deal with facts as presented by the experience of our present world or that of the known historical past.[4] It is a model of a closed, primitive pastoral economy. Its members are pastoral nomads, who entirely rely on livestock and its products for their livelihood and who neither engage in exchange nor practise any form of migration outside their tribal territory. The economy is a closed one in the economic sense only. It exists in a natural environment by which it is influenced and which is a source of exogenous stochastic variations. Such an idealized economy might have existed in a distant past of which we have no records, but as our approach is purely speculative the absence of real life examples is of no relevance.[5] Our present interest is limited solely to the mechanism of the model and its working.

We assume that the pastoral society occupies pasture-lands whose area is fixed but not fully utilized. There is, therefore, a grazing reserve available for temporary use whenever adverse rainfall conditions lead to a deterioration of the ranges previously used. But the fixity of the total area imposes an upper limit on the growth of the livestock population directly, and the human population indirectly. In the case of livestock, maximum sustainable yield stocking density cannot be exceeded, or else rangeland deterioration will force an eventual reduction in livestock numbers to a level consistent with forage availability.

As the size of the human population is treated as an exogenous variable, we accept it as given and can only comment on the expected changes in this magnitude without having to inquire into the mechanisms governing them. It is common knowledge that prior to the 'population explosion' of our modern era natural rates of growth of primitive peoples were very low and those of groups as mobile as pastoralists or hunters were below average. Thus, it can be assumed that growth of the pastoral population becomes significant only over a period of time sufficiently long not to disturb our conclusions regarding the state of equilibrium of the system. Hence, for the purpose of this model population growth is considered to be equal to zero.

Given the size of the human population, livestock numbers can range within a lower limit, which is determined by the subsistence requirements of the pastoral community, and an upper limit determined by the maximum capability of the existing labour force to tend the animal stock. Within these limits, the actual size of livestock population will depend on the level of welfare desired by pastoralists.

A link between the size of human population and the size of animal population is provided by the off-take, which serves to satisfy the consumption needs of the former. At the same time, the quantity and the qualitative composition of the off-take influences the size and structure of the herd. In order to analyse the relationship between the off-take and the herd, let us state that

$$T = T_a + T_m + T_n$$

where T is the total off-take, T_a is that part of it which causes a reduction in livestock and depends on the decisions of pastoralists (e.g. meat consumption), while T_m is that component of the off-take which leaves the herd size unaltered (as is the case with the consumption of milk), and T_n represents losses of animals due to such natural causes as disease, drought, accidents, attacks by predators, etc. This last component of the off-take is, for the sake of convenience, treated as a constant proportion of animal population, arrived at by averaging losses due to this cause over a sufficiently long period of time to obtain a realistic estimate.

Equilibrium of the system requires stability of livestock numbers (P_a), which is achieved when the annual increase in livestock population due to fertility equals the rate of mortality, hence

$$\frac{\Delta\ P_a}{P_a} = O.$$

The last endogenous variable is the cost of producing the off-take. Since the system is a closed one, the measuring rod of money and opportunity costs afforded by the outside world are absent. As there are no alternative ways of providing for his livelihood, the only choice left to the herder is to divide his time between effort of a certain degree of intensity, devoted to herding, on the one hand, and leisure on the other. Effort is the only input which represents an actual cost. Other inputs, such as forage and water, are free goods both to an individual herder and to the pastoral economy as a whole, as it is taken for granted that, at this stage, natural resources are still plentiful.

As has been pointed out previously, the actual size of livestock population depends, among other things, on the level of welfare desired by pastoralists. Apart from consumption, the components of pastoral welfare include insurance against the vagaries of nature provided by livestock, and the desired amount of leisure. The value of production needed to satisfy his requirements has to be set against the value to the pastoralist of the necessary amount of effort. Assuming rationality on his part, he would expand output until the marginal revenue and the marginal cost of his operations in terms of effort became equal. The sum of individual decisions made on this basis would determine the community's total output.

Let us now consider the implications of interaction between the variables. Human population has been assumed to be practically stable. Furthermore, the relation between human population and the land occupied by it is such that, given the welfare level desired by the pastoralists, the livelihood requirements of that population are amply satisfied. Stability of human population entails stability of the labour force. Its size and the desired welfare level determine the amount of effort, in terms of annually available number of man-hours (the cost element), which imposes the upper limit on the size of the economy's herd of the desired species, sex, and age composition.

It is a clear-cut case of the application of increasing quantities of a variable factor, 'livestock-capital', to a given quantity of the fixed factor, labour, which calls forth the hypothesis of eventually diminishing returns. If livestock-capital continues to be added to the fixed quantity of labour its marginal productivity will fall to zero.

The system thus reaches a position in which both the human and the animal populations show a zero rate of growth and, unless there is interference of an exogenous nature, it approximates a steady state condition. The equality between the total annual output and the off-take of the pastoral economy, and consequently an absence of saving, which would lead to livestock-capital formation, are a logical corollary.

As long as the rangeland does not impose a limit, the variable of decisive significance, in this version of the model of a pastoral economy, is the human population. It is this factor which imposes an ultimate limit upon the system's growth.

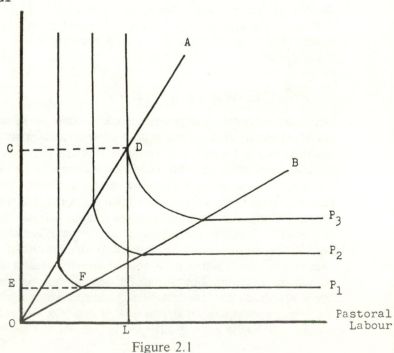

Figure 2.1

This outcome may be represented graphically on a two-factor iso-quant diagram (Figure 2.1). The two factors are livestock-capital and pastoral labour.[6] As a matter of convenience, and without any considerable distortion of reality, we assume that the production process is characterized by constant returns to scale, homogeneity of factor inputs, and fixed technology of livestock-raising. Equal product curves are shown in the conventional manner indicating that output increases as one moves from P_1 to P_2, etc. The ridge lines OA and OB indicate limits beyond which additions of one factor only, i.e. livestock-capital north of OA, and pastoral labour east of OB will not increase output.

Let us assume that OL represents a fixed quantity of labour in the pastoral economy. It follows that an increase in the quantity of livestock-capital north of D, along the equal product curve P_3 will not add to output, the marginal productivity of livestock-capital being zero. There is thus no point in augmenting the stock of capital beyond OC. It is likely that once the limit is exceeded the losses of livestock due to the shortage of labour would discourage further accumulation.[7]

Even if the equilibrium situation depicted in this 'idealized' model may have, at some time, been realized, it has not been maintained.

A 'realistic' model of a pastoral sector

The second model of a pastoral society attempts to achieve a closer approximation to the reality of the modern world than could be attained within the framework of the previous model.

First and foremost, the original assumption of a closed economy is dispensed with. The pastoral society is treated, instead, as one of the sectors of an open economy. For this reason we shall apply to it the term 'pastoral sector'. Largely as a result of this basic change in our approach, a number of corrections will have to be introduced with regard to the nature of the five variables of which both models consist. Finally, greater stress will be laid on the pastoral cycles, so far disregarded, because it had been assumed that the practically unlimited availability of rangeland would tend to dampen their intensity. Attention will also be paid to the general direction of change and the impact of irregular variations caused by isolated events.

Before we deal with the other details of the 'realistic' model of the pastoral sector, let us define, in fairly general terms, its relation to the rest of the economy of which it is a part. It is possible that, at a given time, only some of the links which the pastoral community has with the other sectors of the economy may be present. A generalized schematic representation of these links is shown in figure 2.2.

One such link is provided by migratory movements of the

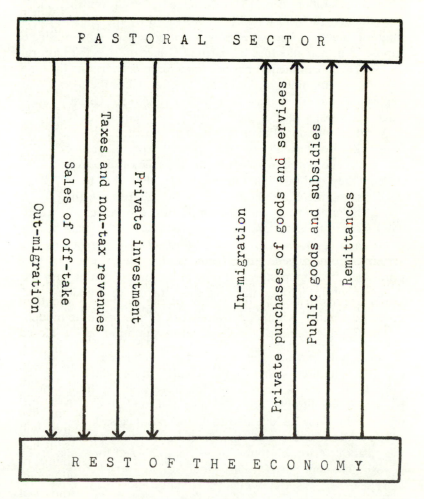

Figure 2.2.

human population which are of a permanent nature, as well as by periodic geographical mobility. Out-migration of pastoralists has been of increasing importance in modern times and can be related to the growing imbalance between population and resources. It is intensified during prolonged periods of drought. However, there is also a strong tendency on the part of the displaced nomads to return to their native environment and to resume their nomadic way of life as soon as material conditions permit them to do so. Thus in-migration can, to some extent, offset out-migration. Periodic geographical mobility is enhanced by the demand for a migrant labour force consisting of individuals who wish to supplement their incomes by earning wages outside the pastoral sector. This phenomenon has assumed large proportions in some pastoral communities in Africa and it often takes the form of an export of labour across national boundaries. Usually such migrants transfer part of their earnings to the pastoral sector.

Another important link is provided by the sales of livestock and livestock products. They are often exported abroad, but pastoralists do not, as a rule, assume the role of direct exporters; instead they act through intermediaries. For this reason their dealings represent a relationship with the rest of their own economy rather than with the importing economies. In many cases sales of livestock and pastoral products are the main source of purchasing power used by the pastoralists to acquire goods and services from outside their own sector. Both exports and purchases made by pastoralists may afford an opportunity for the government to impose taxes. Export taxes on livestock and livestock products are common in African countries and it is likely that at least part of the incidence of such taxes falls on the original producers, that is the pastoralists. Also, the prices of some of the goods and services acquired by them may contain an element of indirect taxation, particularly those which represent imports. In some African countries, mostly in the francophone parts of the Continent, taxes are also collected directly from the pastoralists. They include livestock and poll taxes.

Examples of sources of other forms of revenue collected from the pastoral sector are found in the fees charged for water from government-controlled wells and for government-provided veterinary services, etc., which also include an element of positive or negative taxation.

A further link with the public sector is created by the provision of public goods benefitting the pastoral sector, such as infrastructural facilities represented by roads, communication systems, free-of-charge watering facilities, etc., and finally a range of public goods normally enjoyed by the citizens at large and not identifiable with any particular sector of the economy.

The least significant of all the links is private investment by the pastoralists outside their own sector. The circumstances which increase the probability of its occurrence include highly uneven distribution of wealth and income in the pastoral community or, in other words, the existence of relatively rich individuals, and a significant weakening of the traditionally ingrained tendency to accumulate wealth in the form of animals. In some cases this manifests itself as a preference for investment in assets other than livestock (see chapter three, sect.: 'Livestock as capital and problems of its accumulation').

The above links between the pastoral sector and the rest of the economy affect our five variables, which now require a few adjustments.

In addition to what has been said before about the changes in human population, allowance will have to be made for the fact that mortality rates are influenced by the availability of public health services and famine relief measures. The size of population is also affected by migratory movements. First and foremost, out-migration and in-migration can be linked to the state of dietary sufficiency. Individuals faced with starvation, due to the loss of their animals, will tend to leave the pastoral sector and will return once the conditions have improved and they are able to reconstitute their herds. In some cases, and irrespective of weather conditions, they will leave the pastoral sector, attracted by superior earning opportunities elsewhere. In the latter case population ceases to be a purely exogenous variable.

With regard to the variations in the magnitude of the other exogenous variable, viz. the range, the history of pastoral peoples provides examples of attempts to gain control over new territories by various means. Free movement into unoccupied areas, suitable for grazing, might have been possible in the more distant past. Pre-colonial records indicate that attempts were made to extend rangeland by conquest. Some historical examples of this method are mentioned later on in this chapter.

A question to which an answer may never be known is whether these conquests were primarily prompted by an accelerated growth of human population. From what we know about the demography of the nomadic people it seems unlikely. A rapid increase in livestock population resulting in pressure on the range may be a far more plausible explanation for their territorial expansion. A decade or two of continuously abundant rainfall might have easily led to the doubling or even quadrupling of the herds.[8]

In modern times, previously inaccessible pastures have been made available by well-boring schemes, which represented government intervention involving technology and capital expenditure, usually beyond the means of the pastoralists. On the other hand, enclosures of land situated in the vicinity of villages and urban centres, by farmers, tended to reduce areas thus far utilized by pastoral nomads.

Last but not least, since the range is a common property resource, individual pastoralists tend to maximize its use without paying any attention to conservation measures. This, translated into aggregate terms, leads to overstocking and the eventual, and often progressive, deterioration in the condition of the grasslands. Hence, through the process of desertification, their original area is reduced.

The range and the pastoral population inhabiting it show a degree of interdependence, the only interesting aspect of which for our model is that the availability of the range imposes an upper limit on the size of human population which derives its livelihood from it through livestock-raising. The relationship is indirect, since it must be expressed in terms of the number of animals per unit of area, bearing in mind that in order to satisfy the welfare requirements of the pastoral people, a certain number of livestock per head of human population is needed.[9]

We shall now consider the changes in the first of our three endogenous variables, i.e. the livestock population. In the previous model the livestock per capita ratio satisfied the desired level of welfare. The stability of that level and zero rate of human population growth ensured the stability of livestock population as well.

In our second model, however, difficulties appear regarding the maintenance of a steady livestock per capita ratio because of (a) the appearance of a constraint imposed by the availability of the range, which is accentuated by the variations in rainfall; and (b) the growth of human population.

An optimal livestock per capita ratio would satisfy the desired level of pastoral welfare and, at the same time, would take full advantage of the maximum sustainable yield stocking density, without exceeding it. Under the existing conditions, that ratio is likely to be achieved only as a matter of coincidence, but it is useful as a norm for the assessment of actual ratios. Out of a number of possible courses of action, generally only one has been followed by the pastoral communities with no attention paid to the ultimate consequences. In this particular case the pastoralists strive to maintain the desired level of welfare, disregarding, at the same time, the limit imposed by the requirement of the maximum sustainable yield stocking density. Because of the deterioration in the quality of the range and the growth of the human population, the original livestock per capita ratio cannot be maintained, and eventually it falls to the Malthusian subsistence level. As a further decline cannot be tolerated, forced out-migration becomes a necessity. It can be seen then that, under these circumstances, the condition of a stable livestock population cannot be fulfilled.

So far we have been concentrating our attention on the size of livestock population and have taken the matter of its composition for granted. But from an economic point of view the latter is of vital importance. Within the existing ecological framework, herd composition is governed by the allocation of animals to various uses. Such allocation depends, in turn, on the marginal utility to the pastoralist of the products of which the off-take is composed, such as milk, meat, etc., or goods for which these products can be exchanged outside the pastoral sector. If for example, the desired quantity of milk exceeds its actual supply, the herd composition will be altered in such a way as to increase the proportion of milch cows. Maximization of utility is achieved when the return from pastoral products, per unit of cost, is equalized at the margin. The equimarginal principle applies equally to the allocation of resources between food and non-food goods, which are obtainable by way of exchange. However, the practical application of this principle is sometimes frustrated by abnormal conditions.

The increasing commercialization of the pastoral sector and its response to changes in market prices for meat and live animals, during the colonial and post-colonial periods, have also had an impact on the off-take, which is our second endogenous variable. The off-take of animals for meat may satisfy the pastoralist's consumption requirements directly or indirectly, when other goods are obtained in exchange.

Drought, leading to an acute shortage of forage, will enhance the marginal utility of food in the form of meat, and reduce the marginal utility of non-food goods, and hence the desire for them. It will also increase the off-take by magnifying losses of livestock.

But unlike in the 'idealized' model, where long-term equilibrium entailed the equality of output and off-take, in our 'realistic' model allowance has to be made for a tendency to accumulate livestock. Hence, in addition to the possibility, common to both models, of a trade-off between production for immediate consumption on the one hand, and leisure on the other, there is also a possibility of a trade-off between present consumption and livestock accumulation, the latter being treated as insurance against future contingencies. In a given period of time, then, total output will consist of the off-take and the livestock saved. The approach adopted here is, therefore, to estimate the value of the off-take according to market prices and to assess the costs of production in terms of appropriate opportunity costs, such as wages earned in alternative occupations open to migrant pastoral labour. But the pastoralist's computation of costs includes also the value to him of his preferred nomadic way of life, which can hardly be expressed in terms of money, his leisure, and the relatively low intensity of physical effort, as opposed to the toils of a farmer. Smaller input of labour per unit of output accounts for the attractiveness of pastoralism, just as nomadic farming (shifting cultivation) appears more attractive than fully sedentary farming to those who can have a choice between these forms of economic activity.

The process of change in primitive communities can be viewed as an adaptation to gradually increasing population densities. Its proximate effect upon output per man-hour is to lower it.[10] The experience of many pastoral communities, producing under good rainfall conditions, has shown that in terms of money income alone the profitability of their operations is much superior to that of a farmer. This in itself is a sufficient reason why, even under the rapidly changing economic conditions of the modern world, pastoral nomads cling to the pastoral mode of production, unless forcibly sedentarized, or compelled by adverse circumstances to seek other forms of livelihood.[11]

A partial explanation of the superior private profitability of pastoralism, as compared with that of sedentary farming, can be found in the difference in the cost structure. The farmer's costs of production, unlike those of a pastoralist, include inputs needed for the maintenance of the fertility of the soil. He is also likely to pay a larger proportion of his income in the form of taxes. Apart from differences in the systems of taxation, which as a rule favour the pastoralist, it is a well-known fact that the collection of taxes from pastoral nomads presents special problems and tax evasion is a common occurrence.

A further change in our original assumptions is necessitated by the appearance of a positive rate of population growth, which may double the population within a period of less than half or even a quarter of a century. It introduces a powerful disequilibrating influence into the system. The assumption made in the previous model, namely that the labour force remains in a constant proportion to the total population, has now to be abandoned. A demographic transition caused by an acceleration in population growth rates results in a more youthful age structure and in a growth of the labour force which is temporarily below the rate of increase of total population. Nevertheless, the labour force continues to grow in an absolute sense. The increase in the labour force raises the upper limit on the size of the livestock population, which now moves closer towards the maximum sustainable yield stocking density.[12] As this happens the system becomes increasingly sensitive to the impact of exogenous forces. The resulting changes can be conveniently grouped under three heads: (a) the general direction of change indicated by the trend of the strategic variable, or variables, in the long run; (b) oscillations of various types and varying regularity, superimposed on the trend and responsible for the 'cycles'; and (c) irregular variations caused by isolated events.

Oscillations due to seasonal factors, such as rainfall, which complete themselves in a year are excluded at this stage. We shall devote our attention instead to oscillations responsible for cycles of a few years' duration. The course of a cycle of this type can be divided into two distinct phases. The first is the phase of expansion made possible by a sequence of years of normal rainfall, during which pastoralists accumulate livestock. The livestock per capita ratio gradually rises, since normally the rates of natural increase of the various types of animals held by them considerably exceed those of the human population. For several reasons there is a strong motivation to accumulate. From an economic point of view the most important of these is to be found in the 'precautionary motive'. The precarious conditions under which pastoral nomads obtain their subsistence inclines them to be continuously preoccupied with economic security. Provided that the rainfall is normal and the rangeland remains sufficient, the process of livestock accumulation continues until the active labour force of the pastoral community declines, in relation to livestock numbers, below the minimum required for tending the herds. In actual fact, however, this ceiling is not reached. The time comes when accumulation is arrested by the periodic scourge of drought. Its impact may assume the seriousness indicated by the ravages experienced in the Sahel and in a few other areas of Africa, such as Somalia, in the early 1970s.

Thus the second phase of the cycle is initiated, during which considerable reduction in livestock numbers can occur. The rate of off-take, and the level and composition of per capita consumption, which are determined by it, are likely to be altered. In anticipation of the worsening drought conditions pastoralists are in the habit of slaughtering or selling a considerable proportion of animals, so that temporary glut precedes the ensuing shortage of the means of subsistence. As a result, the existing structure of the herd cannot be maintained since mortality, due to drought or planned disposal, will have an uneven impact on animals. The pastoralists are inclined to dispose of the smallstock first, followed by the species which have the lowest ability to survive.

The bottom level of this process of contraction is far less theoretical than is the ceiling in the phase of expansion. The pastoralists' consumption cannot decline, for long, below the bare subsistence level. Those of them who survive a complete loss of their livestock have to change their mode of life by out-migrating and either taking up farming or, as has often been the case in modern times, seeking wage employment.

When conditions improve a new phase of expansion begins and the cycle continues along a path described by some writers as a saw-toothed history of fluctuations in the size of herds, range deterioration, and a population undergoing periodic famines.[13]

It appears, from the above analysis, that if one ventures beyond the confines of the steady state situation, characteristic of our 'idealized' model, into more loosely defined cyclical movements, changes in the endogenous variables caused by external forces are of paramount importance. But when we consider the occurrences of a more lasting nature, whose impact far exceeds the average span of a cycle, changes in the exogenous variables, namely the human population and the range, will assume the decisive role.

While during the course of a cycle the endogenous variables will tend to return to their original values, this will not be the case with the exogenous variables in the long run. Their behaviour will thus determine a trend.

We have seen that population growth and range deterioration are closely related phenomena. Thus apart from human population growth a source of the disequilibrating secular change is found in the reduction in the area of the range, which may be eliminated from use for prolonged periods of time, or even for ever, due to bad management. Desertification of grasslands, once triggered, becomes a self-reinforcing process. Reduction in plant cover, due to over-grazing, leads to soil erosion, loss of fertility and water-holding abilities. Fewer plants are produced, and if these continue to be destroyed by excessive numbers of livestock, the process is accelerated.

Apart from the trends in the exogenous variables, and oscillations of various degrees of regularity which are superimposed on the former, there are also isolated events whose impact may be quite considerable, and it may alter what would normally be expected from the trend and oscillations of the preceding period. Examples from the past history of pastoral peoples can easily be found and, apart from severe droughts, they are usually concerned with such isolated events of great significance as epidemics or wars.

Early records indicate that the common way of increasing the area of rangeland, when livestock pressure on pastures was felt, was by conquest. One could interpret in this way the invasion by the nomadic Somalis, centuries ago, of the lands along the coast of the Horn of Africa, which forced the retreat of their original inhabitants – the Galla people.[14]

Another example of conquest, in East Africa, is that of the Masai who, from the middle of the nineteenth century for some thirty years, engaged in aggressive expansion and were only arrested by the rinderpest epidemic of 1884. Six years later rinderpest reappeared while, at the same time, smallpox broke out among the people. Three-quarters of the Masai pastoralists perished of famine and disease.[15] On the other hand, the Turkana people, who were not affected by this scourge, engaged in wars against their neighbours, prompted by the shortage of grazing land.[16]

The Southern African episode of the Zulu kingdom under the rule of Shaka, in the early part of the nineteenth century, whose expansion gave rise to extensive warfare and forced migration of whole tribes, known as *Difaquane* in Sotho parlance, illustrates the powerful consequences of a disequilibrium, this time in a mixed economy in which cattle played an important role. There is little doubt that strong economic forces were at work in the case of a population where the success of a way of life, based on farming and pasturing cattle on the range, was reflected in the growth of numbers which, in turn, exerted increasing pressure on resources.[17]

Territorial expansion, unless it involved unoccupied land, as was the case with the Fulani people of West Africa,[18] meant that one group, in an attempt to find a way out of disequilibrium, pushed another group into a similar position. All that might have been achieved was possibly some change in the intensity of range utilization.

But warlike solutions became unacceptable when the colonial administrations extended their rule based on the European concepts of 'law and order'. Unless explicit decisions were made to sedentarize pastoral nomads, they were, on the whole, little affected, as the colonial economic policies and administrative controls extended over them were superficial. Mobility of those people, and the lack of cooperation on their part, made the task of the administrator unrewarding.

In more recent times, government programmes of well-boring have been merely isolated events, which tended to modify the existing pattern of oscillations and trends. By providing new watering points they opened up pastures thus far inaccessible to pastoralists. This form of intervention was often a mixed blessing, as no adequate attention was paid to its long-term environmental impact.

Having discussed the differences between the assumptions made in our two models, it is now possible to analyze the most essential dissimilarity in the way they work.

As our interest centres on the factors limiting potential growth, the significance of pastoral labour has been emphasized in the first model, while in the present model the role of the limiting factor is taken over by the range.[19] A continued accumulation of livestock-capital will eventually lead to the marginal productivity of that factor of production being brought down to zero.

Students of African pastoralism are well aware of the phenomenon of the surplus livestock-capital accumulated for reasons that could be described as not directly related to the present consumption or exchange requirements of pastoralists. 'Unproductive' herds kept by the pastoralists of the East African Cattle Complex provide an extreme example illustrating this form of accumulation.

It should be pointed out that, in terms of our previous discussion of the pastoral cycles, significant fluctuations both in the size of herds and in the availability of the forage provided by the range are quite possible and likely to occur. It follows that the 'fixity' of rangeland cannot simply be interpreted as the total area of consistently uniform quality, but should rather be understood in terms of its carrying capacity at a given time.

If pastoralism is viewed as a continuous economic activity linked to a way of life, then the most appropriate concept of 'fixity' of the rangeland should be expressed as a limit imposed by the maximum sustainable yield stocking density. The 'maximum' must be understood as a safe upper limit meaning that during the periods of seasonally normal rainfall no overgrazing takes place. Overgrazing, in its turn, is indicated by a deterioration in the condition of the range caused by livestock and not due to changes in precipitation. In other words, if no overgrazing is present, range deterioration due to a seasonal absence of rainfall will be a transitory phenomenon. Hence, the notion of fixity of the rangeland is related to the requirement of the continuity of its use.

Cyclical fluctuations and trends result in disparities between the actual stocking density (A), and the maximum sustainable yield stocking density (S). A ratio of these two densities is vital to the system. A situation in which $A/S > 1$ marks a stage at which a danger point has been reached. If the actual stocking density continues to exceed the maximum sustainable yield stocking density a reduction in the availability of the range, through its overexploitation, will take place.

The remaining exogenous and endogenous variables play an important role in the process of wide-ranging expansion and contraction characteristic of our pastoral sector represented in the 'realistic' model. The positive growth of the human population is reflected both in the changing size of the pastoral labour force and in the differences between the desired and the actual levels of welfare. The latter element becomes accentuated when the system approaches its ecological limits, and it is reflected in the growing costs of production. Finally, to the extent to which the pastoralists are in a position to regulate the size and the composition of livestock population, the rate of off-take acts as a mechanism of vital importance.

Conclusions

Whereas in our first model, the 'idealized' pastoral economy appears to be capable of maintaining a state of long-term equilibrium, if not interfered with by external interventions, this is not the case with a model which attempts to achieve a close approximation to the reality of our modern world. The sources of disequilibrium can be found in human population growth, the existence of links with the rest of the economy, and the intensity of cyclical changes. The influence of these factors is reflected in the behaviour of the five crucial variables.

Implicit in this behaviour is also the set of values of a social and economic nature which are the result of an age-long process of adaptation to environmental pressures. From our point of view, the most important value component is the tendency to accumulate livestock as an insurance against the natural disasters represented by drought and epidemics.

As long as the availability of the range does not impose an upper limit on livestock population sustainable by the existing pastoral labour force, the traditional value system can be viewed as a beneficial feature. Nevertheless, with the growth of the labour force, and the consequent upward shifts in the maximum size of animal population, a stage is reached in which the limit of range availability is overstepped. In other words, in the first model the adjusting mechanism acts through the pastoralist's willingness to supply effort, which in turn, depends on his desired level of welfare. Provided that other things remain equal, it is a situation in which private decisions made on a family level are sufficient to preserve the equilibrium of the system.

In the second model, with a positive rate of human population growth, the limits of the available range are attained, but the accumulation of livestock still continues as a result of individual decisions, which are based on a set of values evolved in the previous stage, represented by the 'idealized' model.[20] It is still possible to increase temporarily the stock of animals beyond the maximum sustainable yield stocking density without any immediate visible effects of range deterioration on pastoral welfare. Furthermore, even if the accumulation of livestock is continued and the state of affairs gets progressively worse, there is no built-in mechanism in the existing socio-economic system to cope successfully with the problem. No communal basis for action exists and no social values have been evolved to support it. The social system of the nomads is often characterized by a strong measure of disunity resulting from various group affiliations and loyalties which, as a rule, lack stability.[21]

Eventually the forces of nature take the upper hand and the herd is reduced in size to what the range can support, but in the course of this process its carrying capacity declines and through a number of cycles there is a progressive deterioration of the natural resource basis of the pastoral sector.

The speed with which the evolution of the economy takes place far outpaces the speed with which the socio-economic values of the pastoral community are modified. In the absence of forms of insurance against the vagaries of nature other than livestock accumulation, and better adapted to the changed conditions under which economic activities are performed, the measures aimed at self-preservation turn out, instead, to be those of self-destruction. Moreover, if in spite of the commercialization of the pastoral sectors traditional values favouring livestock accumulation continue to be stronger than the stimulus of market forces, the sales of livestock cannot permanently ensure a rate of off-take sufficient to keep the livestock population down to the level required by long-term equilibrium.

The most important conclusion with regard to the future of pastoral nomadism is that if it is to survive as a way of life and a method of production, outside intervention becomes inevitable. A more extensive treatment of the issues involved in an interventionist approach is relegated to the final chapter, after some revealing facts concerning the pastoral sectors of several sub-Saharan economies have been reported.

Meanwhile, we shall devote our attention to a number of problems related to livestock-capital, rangeland management, and above all to the people engaged in pastoralism and the alternatives they are faced with.

NOTES

1. A common property resource is one that can be used by everyone, for almost any purpose, at zero cost. From an economic point of view common property ownership is virtually nonownership. See J. H. Dales, 'Land, Water and Ownership', *The Canadian Journal of Economics*, vol. 1, no. 4, 1968, p. 795.

2. Some of these broad assumptions are discussed by A. C. Picardi, *A Systems Analysis of Pastoralism in the West African Sahel* (Cambridge, Mass.: Center for Policy Alternatives, MIT, 1974) pp. 212–13.

3. A single herdsman may tend a herd of a largely variable size and consequently the productivity of his effort could be subject to changes. The pastoral people are well aware of this simple truth and they show a tendency to combine human labour and livestock-capital in proportions corresponding to an optimal combination of these two factors of production. The problem of forming flocks of optimum size to be tended by a single herdsman is often solved by 'cooperative herding' achieved by pooling together private flocks of sub-optimal size. A few examples may be used to illustrate these procedures. In the case of the Humr people of the Sudan, a herd of up to 150 head of cattle is tended by a single herdsman. Since most pastoralists have less than the number of cattle to form a herd of optimal size, many herds consist of cattle belonging to more than one person (I. Cunnison, 'The Social Role of Cattle', *The Sudan Journal of Veterinary Science and Animal Husbandry*, vol. 1, no. 1 1960, pp. 13–14. In Somalia camels belonging to close kinsmen are traditionally herded in common grazing units, in the charge of young unmarried men (I. M. Lewis, *A Pastoral Democracy*, London: Oxford University Press, 1961, p. 32). A similar example of 'cooperative' herding from a non-African pastoral community is provided by Barth, according to whom the

Basseri of South Persia combine their flocks to form units which can be conveniently controlled by one herdsman. The maximum size of such units is 400 heads of livestock (F. Barth, 'Capital, Investment and the Social Structure of a Pastoral Nomad Group in South Persia', in *Capital, Saving and Credit in Peasant Societies*, edited by R. Firth and B. S. Yamey, London: George Allen and Unwin, 1964, p. 74). Similar procedures are practised by the transhumant communities of Southern Africa, e.g. the Tswana people.

4. The model may, however, depict a situation which existed in a distant past. It is an early stage of development of pastoral societies whose existence is logically necessary for the understanding of later evolution. This 'idealized' model is meant to be a speculation in economic pre-history.

5. Carl Sauer questions opinions on the original conditions of primitive hunting peoples based on the state of their modern survivors (M. Sahlins, *Stone Age Economics*, Chicago and New York: Aldine-Atherton, Inc., 1972, p. 8n). One might be justified in applying equal caution when forming opinions on the original conditions of pastoral nomads. With the relativity of the notion of 'poverty', with a low standard of living people can enjoy an unparalleled material plenty (ibid., p. 2).

6. Since our reasoning rests on two factors of production only, a question might arise regarding the remaining ones. The output (O) depends on the size of the pastoral labour force (L_p), the stock of capital represented by animals (P_a), the amount of the range available (R), and the level of technique of pastoral operations. We can then write

$$O = f(L_p, P_a, R, T)$$

In order to determine the limits of expansion of the system, in terms of output, it is both necessary and sufficient to show the nature of the relationship between the livestock-capital and a factor whose availability is limited, and which in the case of the present model is pastoral labour. The range and the level of technique are of no interest, at this stage, as the first of them does not impose any limit, and the second is assumed to be constant during the period under consideration.

7. By way of contrast, one may consider a situation when the quantity of livestock-capital fell to OE (e.g. due to an epidemic). Redundant pastoral labour would then be measured, at that level of capital, by the distance between the ridge line OB and the ordinate RD, and would then be equal to FG. That quantity of labour would contribute nothing to total output.

8. Normally the rates of natural increase of livestock considerably exceed those of the human population. W. Allan (*The African Husbandman*, Edinburgh: Oliver & Boyd, 1965, 315–16) estimated that under favourable conditions, i.e. assuming freedom from epidemics and disastrous droughts, the herds in African countries tended to increase annually at rates ranging from about four to ten per cent, or more. Similar rates of growth have been observed in the more recent pre-drought years in the countries of the Sahel, where a long sequence of the years of good rainfall assisted in accelerating the increase in livestock population

(*Surveys of African Economies*, Washington, D.C.: International Monetary Fund, 1968–1973, vols. 1–5, passim).

9. It is convenient to assess the livestock requirements of a pastoral community in terms of livestock per head of population measured in animal units (A.U.). For instance, the data provided by W. Allan for a number of African pastoral societies for the late 1950s indicate a range of 14.7 A.U. for the Masai, and 3.2. A.U. for the Turkana of East Africa (*op. cit.*, 306–7). In his calculation of 'livestock units' Allan regards one ox as equivalent to five head of smallstock in terms of grazing requirements. A camel is taken as the equivalent of two oxen and is counted as two livestock units. His method differs from that adopted by the FAO. Allan's figures were recalculated according to the FAO method (see chapter 1, footnote 20). Once the livestock per capita relation for a given community, and the grazing requirement in terms of A.U. per hectare, are known, the maximum sustainable human population density per, let us say, square kilometre can be estimated. Allan (*ibid.*, 309) assessed the areas required in square kilometres per person by various pastoral peoples in East Africa at 1.3 for the Masai (Tanganyika), 0.8 for the Turkana, and 0.5 for the Somalis (Br. Somaliland).

10. E. Boserup, *The Conditions of Agricultural Growth* (Chicago: Aldine Publishing Company, 1965) 117–18. Boserup discusses factors which may lead to a process of economic growth, with rising output per man-hour. However, the likelihood of the presence of these factors is far greater in farming communities than in an overpopulated pastoral sector.

11. For opinions on the economic superiority of pastoral nomadism see chapter 3, section 'Sedentarization: a partial solution'.

12. A parallel could be drawn between the need for the intensification of human effort in settled farming, and similarly in pastoral nomadism, when pressure on land, due to increased population density becomes apparent. In the case of pastoralism, the deterioration in the quality of the range and the increase in the size of flocks create a need for greater frequency of nomadic movements, which necessitates more effort on the part of the herders.

13. A. C. Picardi, *op. cit.*, 105.

14. I. M. Lewis, *The Modern History of Somaliland* (London: Weidenfeld and Nicolson, 1965) p. 102, and also H. S. Lewis, 'The Origins of the Galla and Somalia' (*Journal of African History*, vol. 7, no. 1, 1966) pp. 27–46.

15. W. Allan, *op. cit.*, p. 317.

16. P. H. Gulliver, *The Family Herds* (London: Routledge and Kegan Paul, 1955) p. 7.

17. M. Wilson and L. Thompson, *The Oxford History of South Africa* (Oxford at the Clarendon Press, 1969) vol. 1, chapter 9; also M. Gluckman, 'The Rise of a Zulu Empire' (*Scientific American*, vol. 202, no. 4, 1960) p. 161.

18. W. Allan, *op. cit.*, p. 318.

19. For the statement of the basic facts concerned with the remaining factors of production see footnote 6, in this chapter.

20. It is here that the logical necessity of the 'idealized' model becomes fully evident. The long process of the transition to the present system,

represented in the 'realistic' model, and the exacerbation in recent times of the fundamental problems does not detract, in any way, from the explanatory value of the first approach.

21. A typical example of this kind of loose social organization is provided by the Somali people; see I. M. Lewis, *A Pastoral Democracy*, p. 2.

Chapter Three

LIVESTOCK-CAPITAL, RANGE, AND THE PEOPLE

Livestock as Capital and Problems of its Accumulation

From an economic point of view, it seems logical to consider livestock as a form of capital asset. The physiological ability to reproduce itself qualifies livestock as an accumulation of goods devoted to the creation of other goods, and thus producing an income for its owners. The generally observed tendency on the part of pastoralists to maximize the proportion of reproductive female animals serves this end. But, unlike most other capital assets, livestock is capable of two important functions of distinct nature: one being the production of other capital goods in the form of new animals, and the other being the provision of a variety of consumption goods. While the first of these functions is instrumental in the process of replacement and net accumulation of capital stock, the second can be used as a form of disinvestment.

Income from most types of livestock is basically realized in the form of milk and meat.[1] In many pastoral societies, milk and milk products are regarded as essential staples, or are exchanged for other foods. Reliance on this form of consumption limits the off-take of animals for meat, which helps the pastoralists to realize their traditional desire to accumulate livestock. But even if their consumption consists mainly of dairy products they compete with young animals for milk, a factor that slows down the process of accumulation. Reliance on milk implies large herds with a high proportion of milking animals and an environment which will allow of a sufficient number remaining in milk throughout the year. In regions with a long dry season milk, produced by cattle, can serve as a staple for part of the year only, and the pastoralists have to rely increasingly on camels' milk and on smallstock for meat supply.[2] The abnormal need to substitute meat for milk consumption leads to disinvestment.

Accumulation, or net investment, involves the creation of more than is being used up during a given period of production. In our case more heads of livestock, of a given type, are being added to the herd than the number removed from it by consumption or in any other manner.

The animals are owned and accumulated by individuals who are members of the basic social unit – the family – and the form of capitalism practised by pastoralists is family capitalism. Net investment, however, should be estimated for the pastoral community as a whole since it must be considered as the aggregate net outcome of individual families' investment and disinvestment taking place within a given period of time. Also, it is only in this way that the changes in the relation between the total natural resources, namely pasturage, water supply, etc., and livestock numbers utilizing them can be assessed.

Before we inquire more deeply into the reasons prompting the pastoralists to accumulate livestock let us, for the sake of analysis, consider an abstract situation in which a society of pastoral nomads relies for its subsistence either on milk, or on meat alone, obtained from the stock of animals which it owns. Both the population and its per capita consumption requirements are assumed to be stable, the herd at the community's disposal adequate, and the technical conditions of production fixed. Given the remaining restrictive assumptions introduced in our 'idealized' model, which have been discussed previously, we can presume that no desire for net investment, in terms of livestock, will be present. This kind of behaviour would be normal for a steady state economy. In such a case, the ratio of the value of capital stock to the value of the net flow of inputs (capital-input ratio), and the ratio of the value of capital stock to the value of the net flow of outputs (capital-output ratio) are maintained equal to one another. This equality is realized within an average period of production of, let us say n days. Let us, furthermore, define the marginal product of capital, represented by livestock, as the current product of an additional unit of capital, net of replacement (depreciation), divided into the cost of that unit. As no net investment takes place, the net return from capital is available for consumption by the community. Moreover, in a steady state the marginal and the average product of capital are equal and continue to be the same over time.

Let us also assume that the pastoralists' present desire for the marginal unit of anything which will be available for their consumption n days hence is equal to their desire then for this marginal unit discounted at the rate of discount applied by them to the future satisfactions realizable in the nth day.

It is apparent then that no net investment or disinvestment will take place if the current rate of return over the cost of capital stock and the rate of discount, which equalizes the pastoralists' present and future satisfactions, are the same.

In his analysis of stationary states, Professor Pigou stated his condition for the continuance of a steady state in terms of the equality between the 'objective rate of interest' and the rate at which future satisfactions are discounted. His concept of interest is identical with the Marshallian definition of the marginal productivity of capital.[3] But in the context of an idealised pastoral economy, which we are dealing with here, which is assumed to be largely self-sufficient and has no credit links with the rest of the economy, the term 'marginal product of capital' appears to be more appropriate than that of the 'rate of interest'.

However, as soon as significant commercial links are established between the pastoral sector and the rest of the economy, an analysis in terms of the Keynesian concept of the marginal efficiency of capital and the market rate of interest appears to be far more relevant.

The conclusion which can be derived from the application of the above concepts differs from the opinion entertained by a number of economists, that in a steady state the rate of interest must be zero. This view was expressed by Wicksell, Schumpeter, and more recently it was advanced by Lerner, who also considered an alternative positive-interest model of a stationery economy.[4] But let us stress again that in order to maintain a fixed stock of capital, the Pigovian approach requires that the objective rate of interest (and in our case the marginal productivity of capital) remains equal to the rate (as defined above) at which future satisfactions are discounted. The Keynesian approach suggests, in turn, that capital accumulation will be stopped once equality is reached between the marginal efficiency of capital and the rate of interest, whatever the value of the latter. Hence, instead of insisting on a zero rate of interest, it seems more plausible to rely on the condition that the difference between the two rates is equal to zero.[5]

In view of what has been said in the previous chapter about the existence of the deviations from a steady state situation, it is now necessary to recall the cyclical movements resulting in substantial fluctuations in the stock of capital and its productivity.

The variations in the rate of discount, occurring at the same time, reflect the changes in the valuation by pastoralists of the utility of their present and future consumption. Thus, the low discounting of the future gives rise to frugality. But eventually, when the period of crisis is approaching and catastrophic drought conditions become evident, the rate of discount suddenly increases. The dramatic change finds its expression in massive slaughter (or during the colonial and post-colonial phases also in massive sales) of livestock, as the existing numbers cannot be supported by the rapidly deteriorating grasslands.

R. H. Strotz, who analyzed the problem of inconsistencies in dynamic utility maximization, viewed 'spendthriftness' as 'inconsistent or imprudent planning' − a typical pattern of behaviour of those persons who 'either through lack of training or insight, have never learned to behave consistently and for whom the intertemporal tussle remains unsolved'. He thought that the incidence of the sharp discounting of the future is a characteristic of the lower-income groups in the more developed countries, but that in some less developed economies this problem takes on its most serious dimensions.[6] However, no evidence is used in order to substantiate this opinion.

In contrast to such views[7] the individual behaviour of pastoral nomads strikes one as consistent and full of insight. These characteristics have been fully vindicated by some modern writers as typical of African people living under the conditions of the traditional rural economy.[8]

The pattern of time preference displayed by nomads has been, in a sense, unique in a world where production for subsistence prevailed. Their frugality reminds one of the attitudes of the early 'puritan' capitalists elsewhere. But the reasons for their behaviour had little to do with religious sentiments; they were primarily due to the fact that they could treat livestock as capital, and that the harsh environment made it imperative for them to accumulate it.

For centuries, prudent planning of livestock accumulation by pastoral nomads produced results which were satisfactory under the prevailing conditions. Fluctuations in the size of herds were unavoidable but they ranged within a safe distance of the ecological danger points. In recent years, overpopulation and overgrazing leading to a progressive process of desertification, necessitate a re-definition of the relevant time horizons. The traditional behaviour of the pastoral nomad is consistent with his own time horizon, which extends no further than the occurrence of the nearest catastrophic drought. But there is another time horizon, far longer than that of an individual pastoralist. It is the time horizon of society at large, and it gives greater weight to the benefits of sustained yield range management.[9]

The views of social scientists on the motives prompting the nomadic herders to increase their herds differ in their bias. The interest of anthropologists concentrates on the conversion of accumulated livestock wealth to largely non-material assets. Apart from the contribution of capital, in its physical form, to the acquisition of such non-material assets as expertise in the handling of animals, skill, and reputation,[10] it is instrumental in the creation and strengthening of the web of important social relationships. According to P. H. Gulliver, who made a penetrating study of the Jie and Turkana peoples of eastern Africa, relationships established by birth (kinship), or by conscious effort (affinal kinship and bond-friendship), gain in meaning and significance when they involve mutual rights and obligations concerning livestock.[11] In more general terms a person's position within his community – his 'prestige' – is determined by his wealth, which is restricted to the principal animal herded. The term 'prestige system' has been coined to describe this important cultural trait. Thus the ownership of cattle is the source of prestige in the East African cattle complex system, where family self-sufficiency is based primarily on farming, but wealth is assessed according to the number of beasts a man possesses.[12] At birth, in death, and at marriage, customs connected with cattle are usually in evidence. The dowry consists of cattle, and their passage determines the family to which the children born of the match belong. Also, an appreciable proportion of the judicial cases involve cattle.[13]

The 'prestige system' in eastern Africa includes pastoral peoples, who unlike those inhabiting the area of the 'cattle complex' raise other animals in addition to cattle. This, for example, is the case of the Somali people, who are prevalently nomadic and raise large numbers of camels in an environment unfavourable to cattle.

According to some anthropologists, the pastoralist's tendency to hoard livestock is an expression of his craving for prestige; economic considerations play an indirect, and a definitely secondary role. Whereas this may be true of the societies practising mixed farming, within the East African cattle complex, the prestige motive in purely nomadic communities may have to be relegated to a secondary role.

During the 1960s several economic anthropologists suggested a new interpretation of the pastoralists' tendency to accumulate livestock, which they called *social exchange* or *transactional analysis*. The protagonists of this school of thought consider that the focus of economic activity is high status, that is control over the behaviour of other people. In pastoral societies livestock is a means of gaining that control, which is a desired good and as such has utility.[14]

An economist's view of livestock accumulation by nomadic peoples is simpler and more direct. An explanation of this phenomenon is provided primarily in terms of a 'precautionary motive'.[15]

Age-long experience has taught the peoples inhabiting semi-arid areas that because of the vagaries of weather, dry-land farming offers an existence far less secure than nomadic stock-raising. The latter has the advantage of mobility, important in the event of drought. Prolonged shortage of forage and water will have the twofold effect of reducing the milking capacity of the animals, which may force the pastoralist to resort to greater reliance on meat, and of increasing the mortality of livestock. If the factor of animal epidemics is added it is obvious that the pastoralist must reckon with an ever present possibility of serious losses.

W. Allan provides examples, from various parts of Africa, of reductions in the number of animals ranging from 45 per cent to $97^1/_2$ per cent.[16] F. Barth, writing on pastoral nomads of South Persia, reports average losses of 50 per cent.[17] Hence, the larger the herd, the greater is the probability that in the case of emergency a sufficient number of animals will survive to provide the pastoralist with the means for his subsistence and for rebuilding his depleted herd. This preoccupation with security provides a sufficient explanation of his tendency to accumulate livestock. Moreover, it explains his consumption habits under normal conditions, which make him inclined to rely on dairy products rather than on meat, as well as his reluctance to sell animals with breeding capabilities.[18]

Security considerations may also be reflected in the composition of herds which favours animals able to cope best with a harsh environment.

Sacrificing the quality of livestock for their quantity may raise doubts about the pastoralist's economic rationality. But economic efficiency involves more than the sole consideration of physical productivity. Where the market principle is weak, and the utility of the goals attainable through social exchange is high, little attention is paid to aspects other than technical efficiency.[19]

The primitive economic process is primarily direct, which finds its expression also in the fact that the main productive asset may be consumed without the necessity of conversion through a market and, vice versa, no market mechanism is needed to effect a conversion from a consumable product to productive capital.[20]

In more recent times, when the process of livestock accumulation tends to exceed the limit of the carrying capacity of the range, and the latter becomes a scarce resource, an activity which fails to control its use violates the considerations of both economic and technical efficiency and precludes the realization of the final goal, namely the survival of the system.

There remains one final point. Thus far our analysis has been conducted on the assumption that, apart from livestock, there were no alternative avenues for the investment of pastoral capital. In sub-Saharan Africa instances of such assets, used extensively by pastoral nomads, are rare, and one has to search for them elsewhere. In his description of the Baseri tribe of Fars in South Persia, Barth draws attention to the inclination of wealthy nomads to invest in agricultural land. This form of investment reduces the risk of capital losses while, at the same time, providing income to an absentee landowner.[21]

In sub-Saharan Africa, land tenure systems viewed agricultural land as a 'sacred trust' of the farming community, and therefore non-alienable. As long as slavery (or serfdom) existed, some nomadic societies exploited farming settlements formed of slaves whom they owned, or serfs whom they controlled. The chief asset was represented by human capital and the means of acquiring it could be found in the risks and effort involved in slave raids and the cost of investment in horses needed to raid other tribes.[22]

There is also some modern evidence that pastoralists spend their spare cash on silver and gold ornaments,[23] which is a convenient form of nomadic hoarding in view of the relatively high value per unit of weight and easy transportability. But jewellery brings no income, and the only possible gain is in terms of asset appreciation. However, this last consideration is of limited importance because a private seller can seldom realize the cost of workmanship. The use-value and esteem-value of jewellery are more important than the precautionary and speculative motives for hoarding it.[24]

Since the domestic production of precious metals in the African countries where pastoralism is important is negligible or nil, the demand for them is met by imports. Hence a misuse of resources occurs, which could be better utilized for the acquisition of capital or consumer goods. On the other hand, it has been argued that imports of precious metals in the less developed countries may perform a useful function when they act as 'inducement goods' for local producers, who tend to increase their marketed surplus.[25]

Trade in Livestock and the Distribution of Its Ownership

So far we have viewed the economies of pastoral nomads in sub-Saharan Africa as largely self-sufficient entities producing directly for the subsistence needs of their populations. Trade has been assumed to be of marginal significance. Its main purpose was to supplement the diet based on animal products with farm produce of a vegetable nature, and to procure other necessities such as clothing, etc. in the neighbouring markets. Under normal conditions, trade would take place if the marginal utility to the pastoralists of the objects acquired exceeded the marginal utility, to them, of the animals, or animal products offered in exchange. Gradually, the profit motive, thus far rudimentary, may make its appearance together with new wants and an interest in new forms of investment or hoarding.

Trade data point to substantial and continuing exports of livestock and livestock products, which in a few cases go as far back as the early years of the colonial period. Case studies of Somalia and Botswana, illustrating the above point, are presented in the chapters which follow. More recent trade statistics indicate that in 1963 livestock and livestock products constituted 40 per cent of the total value of Somalia's exports, and 92 per cent in Botswana (former Bechuanaland). In 1972 this proportion rose to 61 per cent in Somalia, whereas during the early 1970s Botswana's exports began to be dominated by the newly discovered minerals. However, the absolute value of the exports of animal origin continued to grow.

The existence of a marketable surplus may be linked to the distribution of ownership of livestock. If the general distributional pattern is such that the number of animal units per pastoralist is close to his subsistence requirements, the distribution of ownership is not only fairly even, but also there is little opportunity for the creation of a marketable surplus. Allowance may be made, of course, for exchange transactions of marginal significance aimed at improving the variety of diet, etc.

During the colonial period endeavours to maintain the rates of natural increase of animals at a satisfactory level, relied primarily on the control over animal epidemics. But when, due to more rapid growth of livestock population, the limits of the carrying capacity of the range were reached, a further increase in livestock numbers required an extension of the area of pasture land. As already mentioned, investment in new wells was made, thereby permitting additional pastures to be opened up.

Given the supporting capacity of the available rangeland, the alternative method of achieving a marketable surplus is found in the reduction of human population numbers, or in minimizing the rate of population growth vis à vis that of livestock, and thereby minimizing total subsistence requirements.

In more recent times, this aim has partly been achieved by the absorption of pastoralists in wage employment or through the process of sedentarization, whereby the pastoral nomads were turned into farmers. The former solution did not reach large proportions in the economies of sub-Saharan Africa because of their inability to create sufficient employment opportunities. This is true of such typically pastoral economies, situated in the rain-deficient areas, as Somalia, and the countries of the Sahel-Sudan region. Nevertheless, some of these countries, e.g. Botswana, in Southern Africa, rely on the demand for migrant labour in the neighbouring states.[26]

In the majority of cases permanent or temporary elimination of families from the pastoral community took place under pressure intensified by adverse weather conditions, or created by governments, which in some instances by means of forced sedentarization, transformed nomadic groups into communities of agriculturalists.

The availability of marketable surplus of livestock may also be related to the degree of inequality in the distribution of ownership of animals. Given the intensity of the desire for security provided by livestock, families with larger herds should be more willing to sell some of their animals than those which own herds of smaller size. Unequal distribution may facilitate the creation of a marketable surplus of animals, but it is by no means a necessary condition for its existence. Potential surplus is present whenever family ownership of livestock exceeds the combined requirements determined by subsistence and the precautionary motive, irrespective of the degree of inequality of pastoral wealth.

In Africa, data is scanty on the distribution of livestock among pastoral nomads and semi-nomads as well as among settled societies dependent on animal husbandry. Information on the distribution of livestock ownership is, more often than not, based on general observation rather than on systematic surveys. Some insight is provided by the cross-cultural material contained in the Murdock Ethnographic Atlas.[27] In the twenty-seven African societies in which reliance on animal husbandry ranges between 46 and 100 per cent, there were only six where social stratification was absent. Sixteen societies were characterized by stratification and wealth distinction, and information was lacking regarding the remaining five. The comparability of the data pertaining to particular societies is weakened by the long time period during which they were assembled (1890–1950).

There is also more recent and more detailed but fragmentary information in the writings of students of African pastoral peoples. For instance, Cunnison, writing about the Baggara people of the Sudan, observed that in a tribe a handful of men had between five hundred and a thousand head of cattle, and in each *omodiya* (a group of kinsmen) a few men had over a hundred head, while a man with a family had at least a cow and a bull. The general impression was one of a great variation in numbers of cattle owned at any time, just as there was variation in one man's numbers over a period of years.[28]

Another valuable insight is found in Dr. P. H. Gulliver's work on the Turkana and Jie people, whom he described as 'wealthy stockowners'. At the time of his field research in Turkanaland (between 1948 and 1950), though there were wealthy families with up to one hundred cattle and over three hundred small-stock, there were no great variations in the size of family herds. A 'typical' family owned about twenty-five to thirty cattle and about one hundred to one hundred and fifty small-stock. Very few families owned smaller herds or none at all, for existence without stock in the semi-desert Turkanaland is impossible. Their members occasionally worked for more wealthy people or were reduced to the life of gatherers.[29]

In Jieland, with a mixed economy, wealth was less evenly distributed. There was a contrast there between the most prosperous houses with one hundred to one hundred and fifty cattle and those with but a handful. Small stock was yet more unevenly distributed and poorer people had to fall back on farming and trade.[30]

I. M. Lewis, in his study carried out in the late 1950s in the then British Protectorate of Somaliland, included information on the distribution of livestock based on a sample of thirty-six nuclear nomadic families.[31] The data for camels, cattle, sheep and goats, when converted into animal units (A.U.), indicate the following distribution:

(*shown on p. 51*)

A.U.	Number of families
0–100	25
101–200	5
201–300	1
301–400	2
401 +	3

The median number of A.U. in a family was 70, and the average number for the sample was 132.1 A.U. In terms of particular species, the average number of camels owned by a nuclear family was 84.6, and that of sheep and goats was 335.6. Cattle, which are of little significance in the northern region of Somalia, were owned by only five of the thirty-six families.

Professor Lewis thought that a wife and young family of four or five children require a flock composed of sheep and goats of at least fifty to sixty head.[32] There were only four families in the sample which did not satisfy this requirement.

The family ownership of livestock ranged between 4.4 A.U. and 660.0 A.U. In the latter case, the family herd was composed of 500 camels and 1,100 sheep and goats. The variation in herd sizes was considerable.

An example of the distribution of livestock, based on official statistical data, is provided by Botswana, where transhumance is widely practised. The 1971–72 statistics indicate that 38 per cent of cattle owners had between one and ten heads, and a similar proportion owned twenty-one heads and over, whereas 24 per cent owned between eleven and twenty heads of cattle.[33]

It appears that the prevailing pattern of wealth, and consequently income distribution among African societies dependent on animal husbandry, is one of inequality. Nonetheless, because of the tenuous nature of the data no firm inferences can be made. There is, however, little doubt about the instability in the distribution of livestock ownership. What are, then, the factors affecting the distributional patterns and the direction of change in them? As the phenomena in question are of a fairly general nature, facts related to non-African pastoral societies will also assist us in finding an answer.

First and foremost, those few writers who pay attention to the problems of distribution stress the importance of processes inhibiting the concentration of wealth. F. Barth, who in 1958 carried out a survey of a pastoral nomad group of the Basseri tribe of South Persia, points out that greater wealth generally leads to an eventual fragmentation of the household, which takes place earlier in the life of its members than is the case with less wealthy families. The marriage of sons leads to a dispersal of the household's capital, as they are entitled to a share of their father's flock. In the wealthy households the expected marriage age of men is in their twenties; among poor people it is usually postponed until the necessary capital is accumulated. Thus, for the wealthy the dispersal of the flock commences earlier and this is accompanied by the loss of cheap and dependable labour provided by unmarried sons.

In the societies practising polygyny, as is the case with the Basseri, it is common for wealthy herd owners to contract plural marriages. As a consequence, there is a significant increase in the size of the household, and eventually the division of capital required by marriages of the sons and inheritance is intensified.[34]

Some of these factors, e.g. marriage and inheritance, are also emphasized by R. Paine in his analysis of the northern nomadic herders of the Old and New Worlds.[35]

P. H. Gulliver's investigations among the Turkana and Jie throw some light on the African situation. Livestock serves a multitude of purposes and is frequently passed from owner to owner; hence a family's wealth is liable to considerable fluctuations. The mechanism of bridewealth is of paramount importance. Daughters and sisters of a poor pastoralist will add to his flock at their weddings. On the other hand, a wealthy man expends stock upon his own and his sons' marriages. It is generally accepted that a man gives according to his wealth and, therefore, marriages between poor and wealthy have a strong redistributional effect.[36] Redistribution is also enhanced since, as a rule, bridewealth is made up of a large number of contributions, and on transfer it is divided amongst a large number of recipients. At both ends relatives and bond-friends are involved.[37]

Furthermore, there are processes which encourage the elimination from the community of persons deviating significantly in wealth from what is considered as typical. At the one extreme the elimination occurs through impoverishment. F. Barth reports a high empirical frequency of sedentarization of the Basseri tribe through this factor. It was the case for one person in every three in the groups of his censuses. The usual causes of this phenomenon are drought, accident, sickness, or poor management, as a result of which a household's flock falls below the minimal level necessary for subsistence.[38] At the other extreme, a wealthy livestock owner may seek new forms of investment, e.g. in agricultural land. It is not uncommon amongst the very rich African pastoralists to become permanent urban dwellers. They differ in their attitudes from the poor, who settle in the expectation of resuming nomadic life as soon as they are in a position to do so.[39]

In the Basseri tribe of South Persia, due to the strength of the factors inhibiting the concentration of wealth the tribe displayed a considerable degree of social and economic homogeneity within the group consisting of independent and self-sufficient small herd owners. It is unlikely, however, that in all other nomadic societies the above factors act with equal strength, or that they are all present. The nature of their impact is also bound to change as the process of modernization gradually progresses.

Redistribution suggests the existence of a surplus. The redistributive mechanisms of the traditional society utilize this surplus to produce a greater degree of equality. The continuity of an economic system requires that a mechanism leading to polarization of wealth must be equalled by a mechanism that redistributes it. Otherwise the system would be destroyed in an exponential positive feedback explosion.[40] An example of a positive feedback can be found in the profit motive. Once the redistributive forces begin to weaken the road towards concentration of wealth is opened. Firstly, the elimination of the poorest puts the resources previously used by their livestock, such as the pastures and the water, at the disposal of those who can make better use of them. Secondly, further impoverishment of the poor creates a supply of cheap labour for the benefit of those pastoralists who need it to tend their growing herds. Intensified commercialization, by stimulating production for the market, increases opportunities for investment within the pastoral community, which now retains its wealthiest members instead of eliminating them.

Rangeland and Its Management

In the pastoral nomad groups, the pattern which has emerged during the modern phase of development has been one of increasing pressure on pastures. As a result of successful attempts to reduce mortality rates, human population is growing faster and so is livestock. On the whole, efforts to increase the area of rangeland do not keep pace with the change in the two other variables. There is also a progressive deterioration in the quality of pastures due to overgrazing. The familiar cycle of the earlier times – the 'upswing': accumulation of livestock, and the eventual 'downswing': the decimation from natural causes, followed by a new phase of accumulation – now reaches a stage of overstocking, and consequent overgrazing, during the 'upswing'. The relatively mild cyclical movement has assumed the nature of a 'boom' and 'crash' sequence.

While, in the past, the existing institutions were consistent with the fairly stable needs of the group, today this is not the case any more. The basic institutions are the family or individual ownership of livestock, and the common ownership of rangeland. A common property resource is one that can be used by everyone at zero cost.[41] Among pastoral nomads this principle applies to a group such as e.g. a tribe, exercising common ownership rights over a specified territory. Common use of pastureland is open to every family in the group on an equal basis. In emergency situations members of other groups may be permitted to graze their livestock temporarily by reciprocal agreement. The same applies to water resources, except that in some cases persons or groups, who invested in boreholes, may be entitled to their exclusive use. By implication, the area of pasture within a certain radius of the water-point ceases to be easily accessible to other livestock owners.

An asset commonly owned is economically inefficient in that it tends to be over-used, unlike assets subject to more restrictive property rights. This is implied by the common saying that 'everybody's property is nobody's property'. For an individual pastoralist to restrict the use of pasture in order to preserve its quality for the future, or to invest in its improvement, makes no sense at all, because someone else will take advantage of his efforts. But over-use results in deterioration of the resource. No value is attached by individuals to the benefits they derive from pastureland and, from their private point of view, no question of costs arises. However, cost is borne by the community as a whole – it is a social cost. A good which is free for the individual becomes a scarce good for the society. Sooner or later it will be imperative to regulate the use of common pasture, if that use is to continue.

Under common property ownership rangelands can yield no rent, and consequently nobody has an interest in maintaining their quality as if they were an income-earning asset. This can be accomplished only by turning them into private or public property subject to an unified directing power.[42]

One of the case studies included in this book – that of Botswana (see chapter six) – outlines a concrete solution to this problem. It has been accepted as the policy by the Government of that country and it is adapted to the local conditions, a circumstance which restricts its usefulness. Future solutions, in order to be applicable elsewhere, will have to take into account the differentiation of environmental and socio-economic characteristics of the pastoral societies.

In various parts of the world, solutions that have been found in the past ranged from community controls to the creation of ranches run on a commercial basis. Decisions on costs related to improvements depend on the expected value of output. But the assessment of the latter has been, at best, tentative owing to the lack of data and the role played by considerations of risk and uncertainty. Investment in the improvement of pastures is of a long-term nature and the prediction of future price levels for end products, as well as the estimation of the cost of inputs, create serious problems. For this very reason rangeland improvements, whether undertaken by private entrepreneurs or by government agencies within national development programmes, has represented an act of faith rather than action based on reliable cost-benefit analysis.[43]

Planned improvement of the natural grazing lands requires methods which are provided by scientific range management. As a branch of science it administers the use of rangeland with a view to obtaining maximum livestock or game production consistent with the conservation of the natural resource represented by the range.[44] Range management involves decisions on what is the proper grazing use. Suitability of the range for various species of animals or their combination has to be assessed together with their numbers, the season they are to be grazed in, and the rotation of grazing between different parts of the range. An important task is to find the best methods of improving forage yield. This depends on the local conditions and the resources available and relies on such procedures as seeding new and better forage species, eliminating weeds and brush, fertilizing the soil, etc.

Efforts to increase the usability of range can also be made by improvements in the uniformity of grazing use, which can be achieved by properly located fences and proper spacing of wells. Range management should also pay attention to other land uses and ensure their proper correlation with grazing. With the growth of human population rangelands become less isolated and social aspects of multiple uses of land must often be considered. Last but not least, proper care must be taken of livestock, which includes breeding procedures, nutrition, animal health, etc.[45]

But above all, if the task of range management is to improve the already overgrazed range, the disturbing processes must be stopped and livestock control, often involving destocking, becomes a basic condition for success. Otherwise attempts to arrest such phenomena as soil erosion and desertification will be simply futile.

A study of grazing habits of unconfined wild animals has shown that they conform closely with the requirements of modern range management, the methods of which amount to little more than a scientific effort to recreate natural conditions. Wild animals graze selectively, constantly move about, and do little damage to vegetation. The presence of a great number of species results in a relatively uniform use of the range, as they have preference for different plants. Many of them can graze for long periods without being watered and in consequence overgrazing within easy reach of watering points is avoided.

Traditional nomadic grazing methods closely resembled those of wild grazing animals, and until modern interventions distorted the original patterns, they were on the whole well adapted to the ecology of the semi-arid zones occupied by pastoral nomads. The transition to semi-nomadic patterns of land use, by limiting movement and promoting concentration around watering points, led to the destruction of rangelands.[46] Growth of human population has been instrumental in the extension of pastoral activities to more arid lands which, if misused, can deteriorate quickly. In many of these areas the utilization of wildlife resources may be capable of producing higher yield than could be obtained by concentrating on domestic animals.[47]

The experience of range management indicates that better results can be expected from the concentration of efforts on the intensive development of small but highly productive sites rather than from extensive management of much larger but inferior areas. Also it makes more sense economically and ecologically to improve the quality of existing rangelands, even if this implies efforts to reverse downward trends, than to open up new pastures, which will eventually be subjected to the same consequences of mismanagement as has been the case in many pastoral economies.[48]

Grasslands of tropical Africa have been generally neglected and permitted to deteriorate in quality. Unless their deterioration has not gone too far, even relatively small expenditure on improvement per unit of area can be highly productive. There are many examples indicating that relatively simple and inexpensive measures can result in spectacular increases in the returns to the investor.[49]

However, the basic consideration on which all else seems to depend is a system of ownership which does not frustrate efforts to introduce improvements.

Sedentarization: A Partial Solution

Sedentarization is often suggested as the obvious solution to the complex problem of nomadism. But it is an ambiguous term unless a distinction is made between voluntary and forced settlement. It is conceivable that forced sedentarization may be imposed in a situation where the relevant opportunity costs, determined by the free market, clearly tip the scale in favour of the continuation of the nomadic mode of production. From an economic point of view such a change would be undesirable.

Sedentarization is hardly voluntary when the starving nomad's herds are destroyed and he has no other choice. On the other hand, opportunities which exist in other sectors of the economy may induce a pastoral nomad voluntarily to change his way of life.

In the past, government policies have been mainly concerned with large-scale solutions, and the most outstanding schemes of this kind were implemented outside sub-Saharan Africa.

An example of forced sedentarization of pastoral nomads, carried out during the first half of the twentieth century, was that in Central Asia, including Kazakhstan, under the Soviet regime. On the eve of the revolution of 1917, Kazakhstan, Kirgizia, and a large part of Turkmenia were areas where pastoral economy of a nomadic and semi-nomadic type predominated and, up to 1930, nomads and semi-nomads accounted for nearly 70 per cent of the four million Kazakh population of Kazakhstan, the territorially second largest Soviet Republic.[50] Spatial mobility coupled with resistance, originally to the imposed tsarist rule and later, under the revolutionary regime, to the process of collectivisation, made political and economic control over population extremely difficult. According to official pronouncements 'reorganization of the economy of the nomads and semi-nomads along socialist line required sedentarization'.[51] By 1934, in spite of strong opposition, nearly 86 per cent of all farm units had been collectivised,[52] and by 1937 the process was completed and nomadism practically eliminated. The sedentarization of the Kazakh nomads had a disastrous effect on the livestock population, which declined by nearly 90 per cent within a few years.[53] Eventually, it was realized that natural pastures ought to be put again to productive use as these were a valuable asset. Pastoralism was resurrected in a new form of transhumance, under the control of collective farms, and efforts were made to restore livestock numbers to the pre-collectivisation level.

Instances where large-scale sedentarization was forced on the nomads, not so much by compulsory administrative measures as by the pressure of economic and ecological conditions, are readily provided by the former French Sahara and the Sahel in sub-Saharan Africa. Robert Capot-Rey distinguished three stages of sedentarization of the Saharan and Sahelian nomads. In the first stage there is a visible reduction in the extent of pastoral movements; then comes temporary sedentarization; and finally pastoralism becomes wholly transhumant, i.e. limited to a periodic movement of herds accompanied by herdsmen only.[54]

During the later years of the colonial period nomads were settling under the pressure of poverty caused by the lack of animals in quantity sufficient for subsistence. The attraction of a fixed wage paid in the construction industry also played its role. It offered more security than the income from livestock, which varied according to rainfall and the incidence of disease.[55] Industrialization in the neighbouring territories and the discovery of oil in the Sahara were of no small importance and, in some cases, they were instrumental in the sedentarization of entire tribes.[56] In Southern Algeria the settlement of nomads, which for a long time had been a local and periodical phenomenon, became more general and permanent. But large nomadic groups in other parts of the Sahara tended to adapt their way of life to changing circumstances without necessarily abandoning nomadism.

Large-scale sedentarization in the Sahara would require water resources far exceeding those that are readily available. Financial resources of the late 1950s were not adequate to provide artesian wells, housing and equipment for the prospective farmers. According to the French estimates it cost 23,000 NF per family to sink a well, develop and plant the land, and construct a house – an investment which for all Algerian nomads would have exceeded the whole budget of that territory.[57] Hence, the only possible form of existence for some 1.2 million nomads in the Sahara was animal husbandry relying on the extensive use of grasslands.[58] There were no alternatives in the form of mass out-migration.

In the Sahel, where the ecological conditions do not favour sedentarization, as farming requires irrigation and the use of floodplains, pasturage is only practicable by transhumance.[59] The settlement which took place in that part of Africa assumed an unsatisfactory form. The uncertain nature of agriculture north of the 300 mm isohyet, and the low productivity of the soil, forced the settling nomad to retain his flock as a secondary source of livelihood. As a rule, the new settlements were formed either around the government posts, established at watering points, or around 'family wells'. Overstocking and consequent overgrazing led to a decline in the quality of animals.

Once the most efficient workers in the family abandoned herding for some other occupation, the mobility of the group was reduced. This led to severe losses when the summer rains were late and the land around the well could not provide adequate forage. It became clear that sedentarization of this type was undesirable.[60]

Examples of the transition from the nomadic to sedentary life can also be found in Somalia. In the course of the last one hundred years, pastoralists under acute ecological pressure have turned to mixed farming in the north-west area favoured by rainfall. Moreover, many farmers living today in the fertile zone between the Shabelle and Juba rivers are of nomadic ancestry.[61]

A recent experiment in sedentarization has been initiated by a group of Kenyan Somali faced with drought in 1970–71. A group of Somali nomads founded a farming settlement based on irrigation. The smooth ecological and economic transition appears to have been due to the fact that the project was spontaneous, and organized by common action. It survived a neighbouring 'aided' scheme which failed because of lack of water discipline, little interest in communal labour and desertion.[62]

There are different schools of thought favouring sedentarization as a solution to the problems of pastoral nomadism. One school is that of the Middle-Eastern intellectuals and nationalists, and the other is that of the Soviet ideologists. The former finds favour in a number of Middle Eastern countries including Turkey, Egypt, Israel, and Iran. Their political influence was instrumental in the elimination of pastoral nomadism.[63]

The other point of view was incorporated in the socialist planning which has resulted in the sedentarization of the nomads in an uncompromising manner. The only exception was Mongolia – the last among the centrally planned economies of Asia, where nomadism exists in its pure form and still dominates economic life.

The main arguments which were put forward in support of sedentarization were political and economic. Colonial authorities tolerated the nomads and even relied upon their dominant groups. The attitudes of the politicians, whose peasant or urban background was dominated by the cultural values of the settled population, prompted many of the governments of independent African states to settle the nomads. Their aim is to turn a 'marginal' and insufficiently integrated group into quiet and docile citizens.[64] The desire of the governments is to integrate the nomads into the fabric of society. To achieve this aim they have to be modernized and educated. As mobility is the mode of their lives educational services are rendered particularly difficult.

Concern is expressed as to the level at which the nomad will be integrated into society. Past experience shows that nomads tend to become manual labourers or join the ranks of the unemployed, thus contributing to the problems of the slums surrounding the towns.

Those who are anxious to turn pastoral nomads into sedentary farmers believe that pastoral nomadism is merely an early stage in the history of mankind preceding that of settled agriculture. In fact pastoral nomadism is an offshoot of settled agriculture (see chapter one) and it is generally believed that pastoral nomads are far more adaptable to industrial employment in the towns than to farming.[65]

The problem of making the nomads contribute more productively to the national economy is of great concern to the economic planners. The difficulty of making them share some of the expenses of the government is also recognized. Assessment and the collection of taxes present a serious problem. Under the conditions of a nomadic economy only the simplest forms of taxation can be applied, such as a cattle tax or a poll tax. The incidence of the export taxes chargeable on livestock and meat exports falls, at least partly, on pastoralists. But this form of taxation is not progressive and it excludes those who do not sell livestock. The impact of such indirect taxes as import duties and various purchase taxes is of necessity limited by the proportion of the pastoralist's income spent on items to which such taxes apply.

If it is remembered that the pastoralists take advantage of the public goods financed from general revenue and, above all, have a free use of the rangeland which is a national resource, the requirement of a contribution to public revenue is based on sound reasoning. On the other hand, it should also be realized that their contribution to the national economy as pastoralists can be greater than if they became industrial workers, or unemployed slum-dwellers.[66]

Some protagonists of sedentarization claim that the policy suggested by them is instrumental in improving the standard of living of the nomads.[67] This argument raises two related questions: firstly, is it true that, in the majority of cases, sedentarization of the nomads brings improvement in their standard of living? Secondly, why, conditions permitting, do pastoral nomads prefer to continue to be economically active as livestock breeders?

Many experts whose field experience is considerable claim that the level of living of pastoral nomads is superior to that of the farmers. In the opinion of F. Barth, who surveyed the lifestyle of the mountain and plateau nomads in some areas of South West Asia, the diet, hygiene, and health of all but the poorest nomad communities are superior to those of most villagers.[68]

T. R. Stauffer expressed a similar opinion with regard to the pastoral communities of Iran, where the transhumant pastoralists are consistently more prosperous and more productive than their farming counterparts.[69]

In their discussion of the problems of nomadism in the Sahel, O. Brémaud and J. Pagot refer to the results of an investigation made in 1956, which disclosed that a nomad with the low figure of fifty head of cattle had the same annual revenue as an agricultural holding for a family of six, and with a herd of over fifty head the life of a comparable nomadic family was comfortable.[70]

Surveys conducted in the Sahara region found the nomadic living levels higher than those of the sedentary population, in spite of the fact that the traditional way of the nomad had been already deeply affected.[71] The views on the relative profitability of animal husbandry by J. Maquet stress the fact that the cattle yield much more per input of a given quantity of labour than agricultural land. H. K. Schneider, who discusses Maquet's statement, adds that '... some Africans say, cows produce themselves, whereas land is worthless without a lot of human labour.'[72]

Such opinions seem to corroborate the conclusions which one can draw, viz., that pastoral nomads, unless forced by adverse circumstances, find animal husbandry far more attractive than sedentary farming. It also follows that, in terms of the relevant opportunity costs, pastoralism is clearly superior, and the ill-conceived sedentarization schemes which result in the complete elimination of pastoral nomadism are guilty of ignorance of this simple truth.

Opposition to the policy of sedentarization has its supporters.

An outstanding example is the independent Mauritania, where the government in 1960, recognizing the impossibility of resettling three-quarters of the country's population, provided a legal framework for pastoral activities by creating twenty-four rural communities.[73]

As early as 1840, Alexis de Levchine, a Russian, writing about the Kazakhs, expressed his strong doubts regarding the desirability of sedentarization. He believed that nomadism provided the best possible way of utilizing the soils of the arid zone.[74] A century later Professor R. Capot-Rey, writing about the Sahara, expressed similar views to those of Levchine. These views, furthermore, were shared by a number of contemporary social scientists.

Modern civilisation and technological change have an increasingly destructive impact on the state of near-equilibrium which, until recently, made the survival of pastoral nomadism possible. But if sedentarization is offered as an alternative to the pastoral life-style its effects on the settlers should be seriously considered.

A number of countries have reported adverse consequences of sedentarization. Many health problems have surfaced among settled nomads. During the 1920s and 1930s large numbers of them were wiped out by various epidemics in Iran. In the past, the low density of the population prevented these epidemics from spreading. Furthermore, the abandonment of nomadic way of life increased the incidence of coronary disease. The Somali nomads' daily intake is up to 6,200 calories, and in certain parts of the country camel milk is their main diet. Yet their blood cholesterol level is low and heart disease is extremely rare. Similar findings have been made with regard to the Negev Bedouin.

The health of the livestock has been affected as well, and an increase in deficiency diseases and parasitic infections has been reported from the areas of settlement.

The countries which, at some stages of their recent history, were successful in eliminating pastoral nomadism suffered from drastic reductions in the supply of milk, meat, wool, hides, and draft animals, Iran and Egypt having been the most notable examples. In the areas with precariously balanced ecology, indiscriminate change from pastoralism to growing crops has tended to turn them into dust bowls.

Another consequence of sedentarization is the increase of the rate of natural population growth, which goes hand in hand with the increased reliance on carbohydrate production.[76]

Sedentarization conceived as a total and compulsory measure cannot be accepted as a unique solution. It has to be carefully assessed in the light of other alternatives. Above all, its applicability cannot be judged on theoretical grounds alone and empirical studies are required before a decision is taken. As a partial solution, however, it appears to be inevitable because the survival of pastoral nomadism depends primarily on the control exercised over the size of human population in the pastoral sector. Can other sectors of the economy absorb the surplus? Will the pastoralists eventually limit the growth of their numbers to make it compatible with their desired standard of life and environmental preservation? The case studies of African countries, with which we shall be dealing in the remaining chapters, will attempt to give at least partial answers to these perplexing questions.

NOTES

1. Let these be treated as 'umbrella terms' covering a multiplicity of products and by-products, including skins and hides and various materials other than meat, obtainable from the carcass. Some pastoral groups utilize blood for food, which is obtained without the animal being slaughtered (for further information see W. Allan, *The African Husbandman*. Edinburgh: Oliver and Boyd, 1965; 303–6).

2. *Ibid.*, 303, 308.

3. A. C. Pigou, *The Economics of Stationary States*. London: Macmillan, 1935; chapter 10.

4. K. Wicksell, *Lectures on Political Economy*, vol. 1, Part III; J. A. Schumpeter, *The Theory of Economic Development* (chapter 5); A. P. Lerner, 'On Some Recent Developments in Capital Theory' *American Economic Review*, vol. 55, 1965.

5. For the relevant opinions on the relation between the rate of interest, rate of discount, intertemporal choices, and the steady state, see: A. C. Pigou, *op. cit.*, chapter 10, and his *Economics of Welfare*. London: Macmillan, 1924, chapter 2; J. Tobin, 'Economic Growth as an Objective of Government Policy', *The American Economic Review*, vol. 54, 1964, Papers and Proceedings, 1–19; R. H. Strotz, 'Myopia and Inconsistency in Dynamic Utility Maximization', *The Review of Economic Studies*, vol. 23, 1955–6; 165–80.

6. R. H. Strotz, *loc. cit.*, 178.

7. Similar views had been expressed by such time-honoured authors as

Irving Fisher, William S. Jevons, and Eugen von Boehm-Bawerk; cited by Strotz, *loc. cit.*

8. For example: W. O. Jones, 'Economic Man in Africa', *Food Research Institute Studies,* May 1960, Stanford University.

9. A. C. Picardi, *A Systems Analysis of Pastoralism in the West African Sahel.* Cambridge, Massachusetts: Center for Policy Alternatives, MIT, 1974; 162, 167. Picardi interprets the pastoralist's traditional behaviour as a tendency on his part to discount future costs heavily. The question is, however, to what extent is an individual herdsman aware of the gravity and inevitability of the future social costs for which he is responsible?

10. R. Paine, 'Animals as Capital: Comparisons among Northern Nomadic Herders and Hunters', *Anthropological Quarterly,* vol. 44, 1971; 164–5.

11. P. H. Gulliver, *The Family Herds.* London: Routledge and Kegan Paul Ltd., 1955; 42.

12 M. J. Herskovits, 'Peoples and Cultures of sub-Saharan Africa', *Annals of the American Academy of Political and Social Science,* vol. 298, 1955; 17.

13. ——, 'The Cattle Complex in East Africa', *American Anthropologist,* New Series, vol. 28, 1926; 650–1.

14. H. K. Schneider, 'Economic Development and Economic Change: The Case of East African Cattle', *Current Anthropology,* vol. 15, 1974; 261–2.

15. This term has been aptly adapted, from an entirely different context, by M. Karp in his discussion of Somali pastoralism. Karp warns that the analogy with the Keynesian concept of liquidity preference arising out of a precautionary motive must not be pressed too far because of the limitations of livestock when its identification with money is attempted (see M. Karp, *The Economics of Trusteeship in Somalia.* Boston: Boston University Press, 1960; 64–70).

16. W. Allan, *op. cit.,* 318.

17. F. Barth, 'Capital, investment and the social structure of a pastoral nomad group in South Persia' in *Capital, Saving and Credit in Peasant Societies,* edited by R. Firth and B. S. Yamey, London: George Allen and Unwin Ltd., 1964; 71.

18. M. Karp, *op. cit.,* 68.

19. Economic efficiency refers to an organization of production which, given the objectives, minimizes the use of the relatively scarcer resources. Technical efficiency may, but need not, coincide with economic efficiency (see Karp, *op. cit.,* 69–70).

20. F. Barth, *loc. cit.,* 70–1.

21. *Ibid.,* 77–8.

22. I. Cunnison, 'The Social Role of Cattle', *The Sudan Journal of Veterinary Science and Animal Husbandry,* vol. 1, 1960; 17.

23. *Ibid.,* 16. The present author observed a similar tendency on the part of nomads in Somalia.

24. G. Chandavarkar, 'The Nature and Effects of Gold Hoarding in Underdeveloped Economies', *Oxford Economic Papers,* New Series, vol. 13, 1961; 140–1.

25. *Ibid.*, 144–5.
26. The problem of the absorption of surplus labour has been extensively discussed by J. Adams, 'The Economic Development of African Pastoral Societies: A Model', *Kyklos*, vol. 28, 1975; 852–65.
27. E. Bourguignon and L. S. Greenbaum, *Diversity and Homogeneity in World Societies*. Hraf Press, 1973; passim.
28. I. Cunnison, *loc. cit.*, 13.
29. P. H. Gulliver, *op. cit.*, 39.
30. *Ibid.*
31. I. M. Lewis, *A Pastoral Democracy*. London: Oxford University Press, 1961; 57.
32. *Ibid.*, 58.
33. Republic of Botswana, *National Development Plan 1973–78*, Part 1; 22.
34. F. Barth, *loc. cit.*, 75–7.
35. R. Paine, *loc. cit.*, 168–9.
36. P. H. Gulliver, *op. cit.*, 39–40.
37. *Ibid.*, 230.
38. F. Barth, *loc. cit.*, 78.
39. D. L. Johnson, *The Response of Pastoral Nomads to Drought in the Absence of Outside Intervention*. U.N. Special Sahelian Office, New York, 1973.
40. W. Suttles, 'Affinal Ties, Subsistence and Prestige Among the Coast Salish', *American Anthropologist*, vol. 62, 1960; 296–305, cited by H. K. Schneider, *Economic Man, the Anthropology of Economics*. New York: The Free Press, 1974; 105.
41. J. H. Dales, 'Land, Water, and Ownership' *Canadian Journal of Economics*, vol. 1, 1968; 176.
42. H. Scott-Gordon, 'The Economic Theory of a Common-Property Resource: The Fishery', *The Journal of Political Economy*, April 1954; 135.
43. A. M. Morgan Rees, 'The Economics of Tropical Grassland' in *Tropical Pastures*, edited by W. Davies and C. L. Skidmore, London: Faber and Faber, 1966; 166–7.
44. L. A. Stoddart, 'What is Range Management?' *Journal of Range Management*, vol. 20, 1967; 304.
45. *Ibid.*, 306–7.
46. R. F. Dasman, J. P. Milton, and P. H. Freeman, *Ecological Principles of Economic Development*, London, New York, Sydney, Toronto: John Wiley & Sons, 1974; 88–90.
47. *Ibid.*, 84.
48. *Ibid.*, 106.
49. A. M. Morgan Rees, *loc. cit.*, 168–71.
50. T. Zhdanko, 'Sedentarization of the Nomads of Central Asia, including Kazakhstan under the Soviet Regime', *International Labour Review*, vol. 93, 1966; 611, 614.
51. *Ibid.*
52. *Ibid.*, 615.
53. Based on data provided by P. George, quoted in V. Monteil, 'The

evolution and settling of the nomads of the Sahara', *International Social Science Journal*, vol. 11, 1959; 584.

54. R. Capot-Rey, 'Le mouvement de la population dans les Territoires du Sud', *Revue africaine* (Alger), 1940; 232–48, and 'Le nomadisme pastoral dans le Sahara français' *Trav. IRS.* (Alger), 1942; 63–86; quoted in V. Monteil, *Les Tribus du Fàrs et la Sédentarisation des Nomades*, Paris: Mouton & Co., 1966; 57.

55. V. Monteil, 'The evolution and settling of the nomads of the Sahara', 580.

56. V. Monteil mentions the tribe of five thousand Mekhâdma, who settled around the Ouargla oasis in response to the demand for manpower, created by the discovery of oil (*ibid.*).

57. UNESCO, *The Problems of the Arid Zone*, Proceedings of the Paris Symposium, Paris 1962; 308–9.

58. V. Monteil, *loc. cit.*, 581; also *Les Tribus du Fàrs et la Sédentarisation des Nomades*; 61.

59. UNESCO, *op. cit.*, 320.

60. *Ibid.*, 321.

61. I. M. Lewis, 'The Drought in Perspective' in *Abaar, The Somali Drought*, edited by I. M. Lewis, London: International African Institute, 1975, 4. See also I. M. Lewis, *Pastoral Democracy*, chapter 4, passim, and I. M. Lewis, 'From Nomadism to Cultivation: the Expansion of Political Solidarity in Southern Somalia' in M. Douglas and P. Kaberry (eds.), *Man in Africa*, 1969.

62. B. Wisner, 'An Example of Drought-Induced Settlement in Northern Kenya' in I. M. Lewis (ed.), *Abaar, The Somali Drought*, 24–5.

63. A. M. Abu-Zeid, 'The sedentarization of nomads in the Western Desert of Egypt', *International Social Science Journal*, vol. 11, 1959; 553.

64. T. Monod (ed.), *Pastoralism in Tropical Africa*. London, Ibadan, Nairobi: Oxford University Press, 1975. Introduction 173–4.

65. C. Oxby, *Pastoral Nomads and Development*. London: International African Institute, 1975; 5.

66. *Ibid.*

67. FAO, *Expert Consultation on the Settlement of Nomads in Africa and the Near East*. Rome 1972, no. RP20.

68. F. Barth, 'Nomadism in the mountain and plateau areas of South West Asia' in UNESCO, *The problems of the Arid Zone*, Part 2, 1962; 353.

69. T. R. Stauffer, 'The Economics of Nomadism in Iran', *Middle East Journal*, vol. 19, 1965; 285.

70. O. Brémaud and J. Pagot, 'Grazing Lands, Nomadism and Transhumance in the Sahel', UNESCO, *op. cit.*, 321.

71. F. F. Darling and M. A. Farvar, 'Ecological Consequences of Sedentarization of Nomads' in *The Careless Technology*, edited by M. T. Farvar and J. B. Milton, London: Tom Stacey, 1973; 677.

72. J. Maquet, *Civilizations of Black Africa*. New York: Oxford University Press, 1972, discussed in H. K. Schneider, 'Economic Development and Economic Change: The Case of East African Cattle', *Current Anthropology*, vol. 15, 1974; 262.

73. Law of 25th July, 1960.

74.   A. de Levchine, *Description des hordes et des steppes des Kirghis-Kazaks*. Paris: Impr. Royale, 1840; 313–16, quoted by V. Monteil, *op. cit.*, 61.
75.   A summary of the arguments both in favour and against sedentarization can be found in V. Monteil, *op. cit.*, 61–8.
76.   F. F. Darling and M. A. Farvar, *loc. cit.*, 678–81.

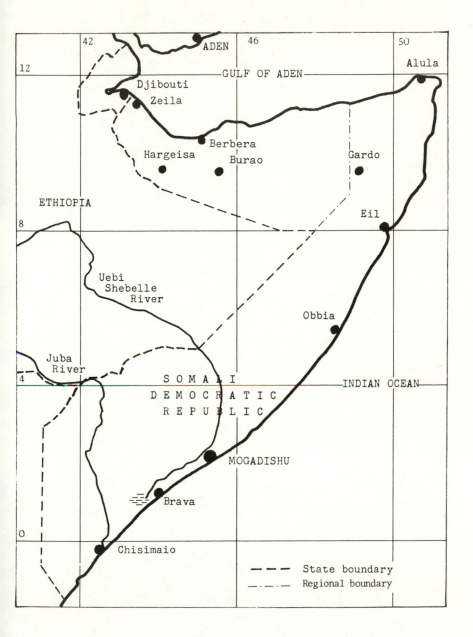

42   ADEN   46   50

12   Alula

GULF OF ADEN

Djibouti
Zeila

Berbera
Hargeisa   Burao   Gardo

ETHIOPIA

8   Eil

Uebi
Shebelle
River

Obbia

Juba
River

4   S O M A L I   INDIAN OCEAN
            D E M O C R A T I C
            R E P U B L I C

MOGADISHU

Brava

0

Chisimaio

- - - State boundary
-·-·- Regional boundary

Chapter Four

PASTORAL NOMADISM: THE CASE OF SOMALIA

Land, People and Their Livelihood

Somalia has been selected as a case study of pastoral nomadism because pastoral nomads still account for a large proportion of her population and exert a considerable impact on the economy. The nature of economic activity is closely related to the climatic characteristics and most of the problems that will be dealt with in this chapter are closely linked to the present stage of development achieved by that country. Somalia provides a typical example of a sub-Saharan country situated in the rain-deficient area, where human behaviour and attitudes are primarily determined by ecological conditions. Unlike some of the semi-arid or arid territories in the Sahel, or in Southern Africa, her economy did not develop sectors such as mining or irrigated agriculture to such an extent that they overshadowed the importance of pastoralism.

Somalia belongs to a group of economies which in the framework of the international strategy for development during the Second United Nations Development Decade, have been designated as least developed. In 1971 the level of most of the indicators, including per capita GDP, was below the cut-off points defined for that group of countries (see chapter one).

The Democratic Republic of Somalia, situated in the Horn of Africa, covers an area of 638,000 square kilometres,[1] which stretches from the shores of the Indian Ocean towards the Ethiopian plateau in the north-west and in the west; in the south it extends towards the plains of Kenya. The shape of the territory of Somalia and its position with regard to its neighbours and main trade routes, have important economic implications. It resembles an inverted capital letter 'L' which results in elongated transportation lines between the north and the south, with an adverse effect on the cost of overland transport.

Climatically, Somalia is a hot and dry country, with mean annual temperatures of 27° to 35° C., intense solar radiation, rapid evaporation and low annual rainfall. The territory above 5° North, is arid, with 50 to 300 mm rainfall, except in the mountainous areas to the west, where annual precipitation is closer to 500 mm. The area situated between the two rivers Juba and Uebi Shebelle has a mean annual rainfall of 300 mm to 600 mm.

Situated close to the Equator, Somalia has two rainy seasons, the major one extending from April to June–July (Gu), and a minor one from September to November–December (Der).[2] Along the coastal strip covering the lower reaches of the rivers rains occur between July and September.

The waters of Juba and Uebi Shebelle, which have their origin in Ethiopia, are utilized for irrigated agriculture. Their flow is subject to considerable seasonal variations. The Juba is a perennial river with two flood seasons. It is considered the main source of water for the country's industrial and agricultural development. The Shebelle has a very erratic flow and it dries up at its lower reaches between December and January.[3] Other water courses are smaller and generally intermittent. Most of the country has to rely on groundwater resources.

Vegetation reflects the pattern of precipitation. Generally it is sparse on the plains and in some places has some thorn bush, orchard bush and acacia trees. It is also affected by saline, sandy or gypseous soils. Along the southern coast mangroves are frequent. Gum and frankincense trees grow in the north-eastern hills in the Northern Regions, especially on dolomitic cliffs.

A rough estimate of the potential utilization of land in Somalia shows that only 12.5 per cent of the total area of 63.8 million hectares is suitable for cultivation, and 13.8 per cent is covered by forests; about 55.0 per cent accounts for pasture land, and the remainder is semi-desert or desert which is not usable.[4]

Conditions for a considerable concentration of agricultural

activity exist in the area situated between the two rivers – the Juba and Uebi Shebelle. The Inter-River Economic Exploration carried out by U.S. International Cooperation Administration in 1960 indicated a potential dry land farm area of 2.5 million hectares, and 12 million hectares of grazing land which had a rainfall of 350 mm annually.[5] Whereas in 1963 only 350,000 hectares were actually cultivated, ten years later that area increased to over 626,000 hectares.[6]

The results of the Inter-River Economic Exploration indicate that there is enough river water available for 160,000 hectares of irrigated farm land. In actual fact only a small fraction of this potential has so far been utilized and a very large proportion of the present food supply comes from dry land sources.

The main islands of agricultural activity based on dry land farming are in the south – the inter-river area with an elevation of as much as 1,000 metres above sea level, and another one in the north, stretching between Hargeisa and Borama, and reaching an altitude of 2,000 metres.

Population data for past years in Somalia suffer from the absence of a comprehensive census.[7] The lack of reliable population statistics has mainly been due to the difficulty of carrying out the counts among the nomads and their continued resistance to census-taking.

A partial census carried out in 1953, in the then Trusteeship of Somalia (corresponding to the territory of the former Italian colony), showed a population of 234,220 registered in the municipal records. This figure was supplemented by an estimate of the remaining non-municipal population. The total thus arrived at was 1,263,000.[8] The statisticians in charge of the census indicated a margin of error of ± 10 per cent, pointing out, at the same time, its tentative nature.[9] The prevailing opinion was that the estimate was too conservative and that a more correct figure of the population for that year was closer to 1,390,000.

The population in the former British Somaliland Protectorate during the 1950s was estimated to be 650,000. Later it was recognized that this figure may have been too high, as it included Somalis who were British-protected but formed the population of the Ethiopian Ogaden. A more realistic figure was closer to half a million.[10] Hence, the total population of the territory corresponding to the present area of Somalia may have been about 1.9 million at that time, indicating a density of population of 2.98 persons per square kilometre.

A general idea of the occupational distribution of the population of the former Trusteeship territory in 1953 was given in the Annual Reports submitted by the Italian Trusteeship Administration of Somalia to the United Nations. According to these data pastoral nomads accounted for nearly 43 per cent, and semi-nomads (i.e. those engaged in livestock raising and farming) for another 28 per cent. Settled agriculturalists formed 20 per cent of the population, and the remaining 9 per cent were engaged in miscellaneous occupations including crafts and trade. In the former British Somaliland the proportion of nomads in the total population approximated to 90 per cent.[11]

Most of the published population estimates must be considered as unreliable. They are, as a rule, arrived at by applying an assumed annual rate of growth to a base year population figure, such as e.g. that estimated for 1953. Rates of growth used in the computation of these estimates seem to be a matter of uninformed guesswork. They simply lack consistency and are not justified by factual information.

An indication of the rates of natural increase of the sedentary population of Somalia in the early 1960s has been obtained from the multi-purpose sample surveys conducted in a number of settlements in the Northern Regions of Somalia.[12] They reveal an average annual rate of increase of 2.0 per cent. It may be presumed that the rate of natural increase of the nomadic population was lower. The explanation of this difference lies in the difficult conditions of nomadic life and a number of other factors.[13]

A population estimate for 1963, of 2.3 million, provided in the Second Development Programme, is based on the 1953 population figure to which an exponential growth rate of 2.0 per cent had been applied. The result of this procedure cannot be suspected of erring on the conservative side.[14]

The plausibility of this relatively low rate of population growth is supported by comparisons with some other African countries where pastoral nomadism prevails to this day. For example, between 1960 and 1972 the rate of population growth in Mauritania was 1.9, and in Chad 1.8 per cent.

The occupational distribution of population in 1963 shows that

60 per cent of the people were nomads and semi-nomads engaged in livestock raising, about 22 per cent were engaged in settled agriculture, nearly 12 per cent represented various services, and the remainder was shared between manufacturing, construction, and other occupations.

Within a decade the nomadic and semi-nomadic population declined from about 71 to 60 per cent, the percentage of people engaged in settled agriculture rose from 20 to 22 per cent, while the proportion of people in other occupations increased from about 9 to 18 per cent of the total. These data support the generally observable trend of movement from nomadic to settled life, expansion of agriculture and the migration to the municipal centres.[15]

If it is assumed that in Somalia the rate of population growth of 2.0 per cent continued unchanged between 1963 and 1976, total population, at the latter date, would have reached approximately 3.0 million.[16] If on the other hand, use is made of a higher, but unwarranted, rate of let us say 2.5 per cent,[17] the result is 3.2 million. The truth may lie somewhere between these two estimates. Population density in 1976, calculated in terms of the lower and the higher population estimate, would have been 4.70 and 5.02 persons per square kilometres respectively.

The data on the Gross Domestic Product of Somalia are of a highly tentative nature. In 1972 the U.N. Economic Commission for Africa had estimated it at US$280.1 million (at constant 1970 market prices). A sectoral distribution for the same year, calculated at constant 1970 factor cost, indicates a 33.7 per cent share of agriculture, 20.1 per cent share of industry, and 46.2 per cent share of services.[18] The difficulties of estimating the GDP in African countries, due to the existence of a significant subsistence sector, are accentuated in Somalia by the prevalence of pastoral nomadism. Moreover, efforts to arrive at a realistic per capita GDP figure are thwarted by the lack of reliable population estimates. The same source of information provides a per capita GDP for 1972 of US$95.4.[19] It is close to the result obtainable on the basis of the maximal population estimate for that year arrived at by the present writer, and based on a 2.5 per cent growth rate applied to the 1963 population.

Livestock

The estimates of livestock in Somalia are even more unreliable that those of the human population. A relatively early official estimate for the British Somaliland Protectorate can be found in the Annual Blue Book for that territory for 1930. It enumerated 30,000 cattle, 1.5 million camels, 2.5 million sheep and 2.0 million goats, equivalent to a total of 2.1 million animal units, or 6.1 A.U. per inhabitant, assuming that the population of the Protectorate numbered 347,000.[20] Another assessment was carried out by J. A. Hunt, during the general survey of the Somaliland Protectorate in 1951.[21] The number of cattle quoted there is 223,000, a figure much higher than that of 1930. The numbers of other animals appear to be fairly close to those included in the earlier estimate, viz. 1.2 million camels, 2.4 million sheep, and 1.6 million goats, equal to 1.5 million animal units. Assuming that, at that time, the human population of the Protectorate did not exceed half a million, we obtain a figure of three animal units per head, i.e. only one half of the 1930 level.

The next estimate was published in the Report for Somaliland Protectorate for the years 1956 and 1957.[22] The domestic animals of the Protectorate included about 250,000 cattle, between 2.0 and 4.0 million camels, 6.0 million sheep, and 2.0 million goats. The disparity between this estimate and Hunt's figures may be partly explained by the fact that the 1956 assessment included animals owned by the nomads who spent several months of each year with their livestock outside the Protectorate's boundaries. If a lower figure for camels is accepted (two million), 3.2 million animal units are obtained, or approximately 6.4 units per capita.

With regard to the former Italian colony of Somalia, we have an early estimate of livestock population prepared around 1910. At that time cattle numbered 840,000 heads, camels 1.3 million, sheep 640,000, and goats 2.9 million. These figures are not comparable with later estimates because of the territorial changes which took place during the 1920s.[23]

We shall now consider the pre-independence assessments of livestock population made during the period of the U.N. Trusteeship Administration. The first of these was for the year 1952.[24] Cattle were estimated at 842,000, camels at 1.3 million, sheep at 600,000, and goats at 2.9 million heads, equivalent to 2.5 million animal units.

The second estimate, prepared for 1955, recorded an increase in all the categories of animals. In terms of animal units animal population grew by 12 per cent over the three year period. At that time there were approximately 1.9 A.U. per head of human population – a proportion substantially lower than in the Somaliland Protectorate during the 1950s. This disparity can be partly explained by a far larger proportion of settled agriculturalists and townspeople in the South, who possessed less livestock.

The next assessment refers to the post-colonial years, and it covers the combined territory of the former Somaliland Protectorate and the U.N. Trusteeship of Somalia. The approximate livestock population suggested by that estimate was as follows: cattle 1.2 million, camels 2.5 million, sheep 3.0 million, and goats 4.5 million. This represented 4.5 million animal units or 1.9 A.U. per capita. The above estimate arouses suspicion as being unduly conservative, particularly as there were no indications of any marked reduction in the numbers of animals. On the contrary, the observed deterioration of the range pointed rather to a considerable increase in livestock population.[26]

In June and July of 1964, aerial surveys performed by low-flying aircraft were carried out, with the purpose of obtaining estimates of livestock population. The results were based on sample counts performed for the project area comprising 208,500 square kilometres and covering the inter-river lands. The human population of the survey area was estimated at 1,285,000. Of this population 38 per cent were classified as partly agriculturalists and stockraisers, 39 per cent as pastoral nomads, and 23 per cent as urban dwellers.[27] Approximately 40 per cent of the cattle in the project area were owned by cultivators.[28]

The total estimate for the survey area disclosed a cattle population of 1,221,000, with a possible range at 95 per cent accuracy, of about 200,000 heads. This was an increase of about 64 per cent over the 1952 total for the area. Camels were estimated at 640,000 with a range of about 110,000. This estimate was 40 per cent less than the 1952 total. The estimated number of sheep and goats (the latter predominated) was 1,601,000 with a possible range of about 340,000 animals.[29]

The results of the 1964 survey indicate that, compared with the livestock situation in 1952, there was a marked shift on the part of the livestock owners from reliance on camels, sheep and goats to cattle.

An official estimate, closest to the disastrous drought years of the early 1970s, had been prepared by the Somali Livestock Development Agency for the year 1970.[30] It reported 3.0 million cattle, 2.5 million camels, and 15.0 million sheep and goats, or 6.7 million animal units. With the human population of Somalia estimated on the basis of 2.0 and 2.5 per cent annual growth rates, we obtain 2.6 A.U. and 2.4 A.U. per capita respectively.

The wide disparities between the livestock estimates for various years present a perplexing problem. If such disparities are due to a high degree of inaccuracy then they are clearly irreconcilable. Cattle and camel statistics are difficult to collect due to the extensive migratory movements within the country, as well as across the borders into Ethiopia and Kenya. To some extent such movements are also characteristic of sheep and goats. But considerable disparities may also be the result of changing weather conditions, or epidemics. Provided that an estimate is fairly accurate it is likely to be meaningful only for the year for which it had been prepared, since interpolations or projections based on an assumed rate of growth are not reliable.

In conclusion, livestock population estimates should be approached with great caution.

Commercialization of the Pastoral Sector

Anthropologists who wrote about pastoral societies emphasized the pastoral nomad's tendency to accumulate livestock as a security measure and as a means of gaining prestige. The economic value of the latter is created by interpersonal relations maintained through a system of reciprocal rights in respect of domestic animals.[31] One could infer from this the pastoralist's reluctance to sell livestock, or even to slaughter it in order to provide food for his household. Instead, he would rely chiefly on milk and its products. Such opinions are undoubtedly true, but their applicability is a matter of degree, and they are subject, therefore, to a number of important reservations and corrections. Firstly, attitudes change with weather conditions. In Somalia and elsewhere under similar climatic conditions, a prolonged period of drought will force the nomads to sell a large proportion of their livestock. But it may occur only once in a number of years. Normally, however, their willingness to part with livestock increases during the dry seasons and it disappears during the wet seasons when pastures improve. 'Good rains in the interior' explains a British consular report for 1891–2, on the trade of the Somali Coast Protectorate, 'bring aboundance of grass, hence milk and ghee are plentiful and the Somali is satisfied, and asks for a smaller supply of food grains and dates ...'[32] Secondly, it is important to realize that, as a rule, pastoral nomads keep only productive animals. And here sex, fertility and age are of decisive importance. Herds are mostly composed of fertile females and of a limited number of males necessary for breeding. In the case of cattle and camels an allowance may also have to be made for the beasts of burden. Infertile females and old animals of both sexes, as well as the young but redundant males, are disposed of. Hence, the 'unproductive' animals provide a disposable surplus. Furthermore, the pastoralist's decisions to slaughter or to sell his animals depend on the species of which his herd is composed.

Apart from the prestige value he may attach to his cattle or his camels, or their usefulness as the beasts of burden, he has to take into account the dressed meat equivalent, or alternatively, in the case of a sale of live animals, the sum of money he will be paid for them. If he slaughters a beast in order to satisfy the immediate needs of his household it makes quite a difference, under the conditions of tropical climate, whether he sacrifices a cow or a sheep, as the former represents an average weight of 180 kilograms and the latter provides only about 22 kilograms of dressed meat.[33] And last but not least, the herder's willingness to part with his livestock depends on the price he can get for it and on the marketing facilities available to him.

Writing on the eve of Somalia's independence, about the prospects of that country's livestock trade, Mark Karp[34] characterized marketing, transport, and port facilities there, as falling far short of what would be required to handle a large volume of trade. He also found that the conditions of demand necessary for the development of that country's livestock resources were absent. A suggestion that even if demand were to improve, commercialization would be thwarted by the Somali herder's reluctance to sell livestock, was not entirely dismissed by him. At the same time, however, he did not exclude the possibility that under the stimulus of a strong demand the Somali pastoralists might follow the wartime example of Kenya and Uganda where African herders overreacted to the soaring demand for meat and other livestock products. It may be presumed that these herders were quick to recognize that high money incomes would provide them with a far greater degree of security than that which they could achieve by hoarding livestock.[35]

It will be seen from the ensuing discussion that Karp's guarded optimism had been more than confirmed, during the 1960s, by the dramatic development of Somalia's livestock trade.

In more recent years attitudes towards livestock do not confirm the views held regarding the Somali herder's 'well known' reluctance to sell his animals.[36] Before we deal with the present let us examine a few recorded facts which throw more light on his attitudes in a more distant past. There is some evidence of continuing exports of livestock, skins and hides of domestic animals from the ports of northern Somaliland in the nineteenth and early twentieth centuries. The principal ports were Berbera and Zeila. Reports of European travellers provide early estimates of trade. For example, in 1840, d'Héricourt lists commodities exported from Berbera and includes among them 8,000 hides and 9,000 sheep and goat skins.[37] During the second half of the nineteenth century Berbera and a few smaller ports on the northern coast of Somaliland supplied all the livestock consumed by the British garrison and the inhabitants of Aden. In 1883 a British official H.M. Durand stated that '... Berbera with its dependent port of Bulhar ... can furnish an almost inexhaustible number of sheep and large quantities of cattle which cannot be easily obtained elsewhere. Livestock to the annual value of 160,000 rupees is exported now from Berbera and Bulhar.'[38] Even if this statement grossly exaggerates the potential, it draws attention to what can be taken as the nomad's readiness to sell livestock. During the same year, shipments from Berbera to Aden included 1,239 head of cattle and 15,605 head of sheep and goats in addition to 23,680 hides and 36,100 skins.[39] A year later shipments in Khedival steamers from Zeila to Aden comprised 9,360 hides and 20,540 skins.[40] Though trade and shipping were largely carried on by the Indians, the Somalis and the Arabs were active in the export of cattle from which the Indians refrained for religious reasons.[41]

The trade of the ports of the northern Somali coast was stimulated by the development of the port of Aden under the British administration.[42] In the second half of the nineteenth century it became an important naval base and commercial centre which attracted a number of foreign firms. Transactions in hides and skins were enhanced by the demand on the part of the resident European and American traders.[43] It should be realized that only part of these exports originated in the territory which in 1887 was proclaimed the British Protectorate of Somaliland. Until the establishment of port facilities in Jibuti and Tajurah, the foreign trade of most of eastern and southern Ethiopia was carried on mostly through Berbera and Zeila.[44] In the middle of the nineteenth century caravans from Ogaden and Harar were bringing, among other goods, quantities of cattle, hides and skins.[45]

From the beginning of the twentieth century statistics of foreign trade of the Protectorate had been compiled annually. They indicate the importance of sheep and goats exported, as compared to cattle and camels. There were considerable fluctuations in numbers exported which, in all likelihood, were related to changing weather conditions. In 1901–2 sheep and goats that were exported numbered 60,000. By 1926, their number more than doubled to fall again in 1929 to the 1901–2 level.

During the 1930s numbers exported ranged from 76,000 to 136,000. Sheep and goat skins exports ranged from 806,000 in 1921 to as high as 1,849,000 in 1934 – it was the highest pre-war figure.[46] During the inter-war period the combined value of exports of live sheep and goats and sheep and goat skins often exceeded two-thirds or even three-quarters of the total value of exports of domestic origin. For most of the 1950s this proportion was close to 95 per cent, which indicated a complete dependence of that territory's economy on pastoral nomadism.[47]

The estimate of sheep and goat population for 1956–7 and the corresponding export data for live animals and skins allow us to arrive at the off-take figure, which for 1957 was 26 per cent. It may be presumed that an unknown proportion of sheep and goats slaughtered for local consumption remained unrecorded, as the skins may have been used locally or wasted, and statistics of internal meat trade were non-existent. Assuming that the local consumption of mutton and goat meat was limited solely to what can be inferred from the number of skins exported, it amounted in 1956 to nearly 80 kilograms per head of population.[48] In 1956 exports of live small-stock were comparatively low, while exports of skins were somewhat better than in other years. Even if it is assumed that the consumption of beef and camel meat was negligible, per capita consumption of mutton and goat meat of that magnitude appears quite formidable for a population whose eating habits were believed to be frugal. The off-take figure of 26 per cent, which was not unusual in the 1950s, makes one doubtful whether in fact the Somali herders lack the willingness to either sell or slaughter their animals for meat. There is also nothing to indicate a rather recent and dramatic change of attitude to livestock.

A similar calculation for 1931, for which we have fairly reliable data, reveals an off-take of over 24 per cent of sheep and goats, and a per capita consumption of 62.7 kilograms of the meat of these animals.[49]

With regard to the southern parts of Somalia we have only fragmentary information relating to the pre-colonial period. The three principal ports on the Benadir coast through which the export trade passed were Mogadishu, Merca, and Brava. The goods traditionally traded there came partly from the interior encompassing parts of the Ethiopian territory, and from the Somali coastal area. According to M. Guillain, who visited Somalia in the middle of the nineteenth century, Mogadishu exports included between 40,000 and 60,000 skins, apart from live cattle, camels and a variety of other goods.[50] More accurate export data became available at the end of the century after the Italian occupation. In 1896–7, exports of cattle, camels, and goats amounted to 9.9 per cent, and those of ox and camel hides and goat skins to 13.9 per cent of the value of total exports of Benadir.[51]

In 1913–14, Italian Somalia's exports of animals consisted of 1,794 head of cattle and 7,704 sheep, and animal products included 243,000 sheep skins.[52] Ten years later, when Somalia was entering a stage of accelerated development of its plantation agriculture, 'pastoral' products constituted 14.8 per cent of the total value of exports. These consisted chiefly of hides and skins, cattle, camels and small-stock.[53] In 1938, the last normal year before the outbreak of the Second World War, skins represented 8.1 per cent, while the most important export of the Colony was bananas – followed by cotton, which reached 42.4 and 20.4 per cent of the total value of exports respectively.[54]

On the whole, during the colonial period the primary objective of pastoral nomads and semi-nomads in the Italian part of the country was self-subsistence. The production for exchange was only marginal. The scope of the transactions in domestic animals was extremely limited. Sales of cattle consisted chiefly of unproductive cows, old bulls incapable of performing reproductive services, and oxen unsuitable as beasts of draught.

The situation with regard to exports of animal origin was not much different in 1954. By that year some measure of reconstruction had been achieved after the desolations and the disorganization of the war. It was also the time when, after the transition from British occupation to the U.N. Trusteeship Administration, a vigorous developmental effort was in progress. In 1954 the exports of hides and skins amounted to 8.5 per cent and those of live animals to an insignificant proportion of 1.8 per cent of the total value of exports. At the same time exports of bananas reached the unprecedented level of 70 per cent.[55]

When considering the relative significance of the trade in livestock and its products in the former Italian Somalia, the difference in the composition of the herds should be emphasized. While in British Somaliland small-stock played an important role, in the South cattle and camels dominated the scene and consequently milk and its products were assuming a greater importance. Moreover, in the inter-river area conditions were favourable to settled farming and plantation economy, which during the inter-war period developed fairly rapidly, adding new products such as cotton and later on bananas, as well as various other crops suitable for local consumption. This tended to lessen reliance on domestic animals. In British Somaliland, instead, no exports other than livestock and its products ever assumed importance and no significant quantities of other foodstuffs were locally produced to supplement the diet of its inhabitants.

Between 1954 and 1959 there was a threefold increase in the

value of exports from the territory of the former Italian Somalia. It was largely due to the revival of the production of bananas for which there was an assured market in Italy. During this short period the share of exports of live animals in the total value of exports rose from 1.8 to 4.3 per cent and their total weight trebled.[56] During the same period, in the British Protectorate of Somaliland the increase in the value of exports of livestock reached 76 per cent, while animal units exported rose by 40 per cent.[57] Sharp increase in both the absolute and relative value of livestock exports, as well as in their physical quantities, continued during the early 1960s. From 1961 to 1964 there was an uninterrupted and rapid growth in both the value of livestock exports and the numbers of animal units exported. The former showed an increase of 111.8 per cent, and the latter rose by 85.5 per cent during the years under consideration. However, in 1965 a substantial decline occurred in the value realized, as well as in the quantities sold. It was attributable to drought. The years which followed were characterized by positive and fast growth, which lasted until the end of the decade. By 1969 the value of livestock exports and their volume in terms of metric tons rose by 27.2 and 34.5 per cent respectively over their 1964 level.[58] It appears then that in the 1960s Somali pastoralists responded promptly to the stimulus of the demand generated primarily in the oil-rich Arab countries, among which Saudi Arabia represented the principal market. In 1966 that country alone absorbed nearly one-third of the total value of Somalia's exports and as much as 70 per cent of the value of her livestock exports.[59]

The problem of resources necessary to expand the supply had partly been solved during the 1950s by the Trusteeship Administration. The investment made within the development programme aimed at the creation of new water resources for agricultural purposes, including pastoralism. In particular, efforts were made to reduce the damage resulting from overstocking on the pastures situated in the vicinity of the permanent sources of water. Furthermore, the area of pastureland was extended by opening up pastures inaccessible to livestock during the dry seaons because of the lack of watering facilities. Between the years 1954 and 1960 some 109 wells were dug, which were capable of watering 27,000 head of cattle and another 132 wells were drilled which provided water to 262,000 head of cattle per day. Water resources available to livestock had also been increased with the provision of reservoirs situated in natural depressions, in which river and rain water was being collected. Altogether, the supply of water available to livestock had been augmented by some 13.8 million litres per day, capable of watering approximately 700,000 head of cattle.

Efforts were also made to control the utilization of pastures. Two projects were started, one in the district of Burao, in the British Protectorate, and the second in the South in the vicinity of Afmadu (Lower Juba), under the guidance of American experts. Unfortunately both these experiments proved unsuccessful because local population did not agree to the limitations in the use of range required by its rational management.[60]

With the coming of political independence the North and the South of Somalia were merged into one country, and so were the statistics of foreign trade. However, until 1965 separate figures for the value of livestock exports are available for the two regions, corresponding to the former U.N. Trusteeship territory and British Somaliland.[61] It is, therefore, possible to compare the contribution of each territory, during that limited period, to the total value of livestock exports for the whole of Somalia.

From 1954 to 1965 the Northern Regions contributed between 86.2 and 92.8 per cent of the combined value of livestock exports of Somalia, thus by far outstripping the contribution of the rest of the country. The data pertaining to the period 1954–65 indicate that in spite of a marked absolute increase in the value and the physical volume of livestock exports from the Southern Regions it did not improve its position vis-à-vis the North. In order to explain this state of affairs several factors should be considered. Our conclusions, so far, have been based on the official statistics of foreign trade. But it is a well-known fact, in that part of Africa, that apart from the livestock exports recorded by the customs authorities, there had been considerable illegal export of animals on the hoof across the borders, particularly to Kenya, where prices were favourable.[62] Moreover, there is the possibility that in the South, where population is larger and is becoming increasingly urbanized, the local demand for meat tends to absorb part of the increase in livestock. Efforts were also made during the 1960s to develop industries producing meat products for export. The evidence, which cannot be doubted, is provided by the

Diagram 4.1 Somalia, Southern Regions, Livestock Slaughtered, 1951–1963

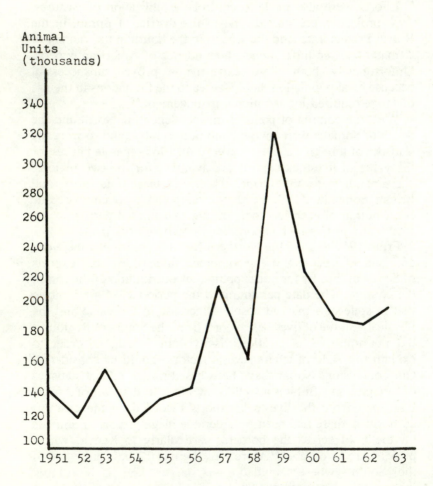

Sources: Rapporti dell'Amministrazione Fiduciaria Italiana della Somalia; Government Veterinary Services.

figures of animals slaughtered. They are based on the statistics of the municipal abattoirs and estimates of animals slaughtered outside slaughter-houses. A striking feature of the time series which provides this information for the period 1951–63, is a marked increase in the absolute numbers of cattle and small-stock slaughtered during the late 1950s and early 1960s.

The total number of cattle slaughtered during the second quinquennium of the 1950s showed a 43.5 per cent increase over the corresponding figure for the first five years of that decade. A similar comparison for the sheep and goats discloses a 103.5 per cent increase, but at the same time a 37.7 per cent decrease in the number of camels. However, the latter played a minor role in the total meat supply. In terms of animal units the second quinquennium's total shows a 57.6 per cent increase over the first quinquennium's total.

The evidence of an increase in the exports of livestock and a marked rise in the local consumption of meat, even if not conclusive, strengthens the hypothesis of positive effects of investment in pastoral resources.[63] The presumed rapid growth in the supply of animals is understandable during the second half of the decade, when the augmented watering facilities and extended areas of rangeland could produce the desired results.

Finally, let us briefly examine the proportion represented by livestock in Somalia's exports vis-à-vis that of bananas, another commodity vital to the foreign trade of that country. From 1960 to 1966 Somalia had a typical 'duoexport' economy based on livestock and bananas. These two commodities accounted for over two-thirds of the total value of domestic exports and neither of them became preponderant. However, in 1966 the exports of live animals and livestock products began to play a dominating role, having exceeded 50 per cent of the total value of exports. The proportion continued to increase and by 1972 it reached 67.5 per cent. Meanwhile, the banana exports decreased to approximately one-quarter of the total value of exports towards the end of the period. From 1966 there was a marked decrease both in the quantities of banana exports and their unit price. A mild recovery took place in 1970 and it continued until 1972 – the last year for which reliable data are available at the time of writing.

Diagram 4.2 Somalia: Value of Total Exports, 1961–1972

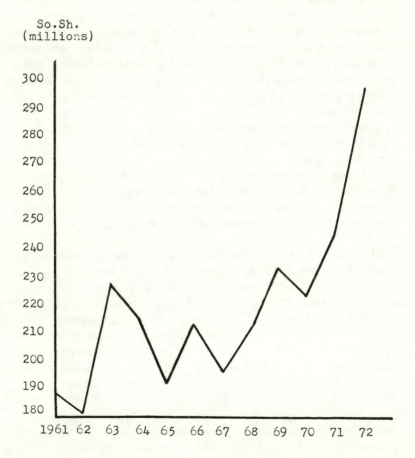

Source: Somali Democratic Republic, Statistical Abstracts.

Diagram 4.3 Somalia: Exports of Live Animals, Livestock
Products, Bananas, and Other Commodities as
Percentage of Value of Total Exports, 1961–1972

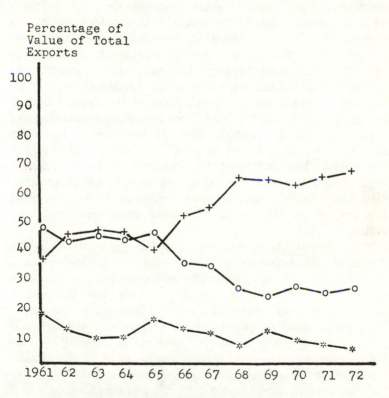

+   Live Animals and Livestock Products
o   Bananas
*   Other Commodities
Source: Somali Democratic Republic, Statistical Abstracts.

On the other hand, throughout the 1960s the exports of live animals and livestock products maintained their price levels and, except for a few years, they exhibited a moderate increase in physical quantities. The crux of the matter was that the two commodities differed in three vital respects with regard to their marketability. Firstly, the income elasticity of the demand for bananas was lower than that for meat. Secondly, whereas livestock was sold chiefly to the Arab countries situated nearby, bananas had to be sent to Europe in refrigerated ships. In the highly competitive international banana market Somalia had little choice but to take advantage of a privileged position in Italy which she enjoyed for many years. Originally she benefitted from the arrangements made with the Italian Banana Monopoly[64] and subsequently from her status as an associate member state of the European Common Market. Somalia's relatively high cost of production and transportation left her with practically no alternative markets, and she had to accept conditions imposed by Italy, which continued to absorb most of the Somali output. Thirdly, the closure of the Suez Canal increased the problems of banana exports. By contrast, sales of livestock to the Arab countries were stimulated by Somalia's comparative advantage in that market. The preference for live animals rather than for dressed meat can be explained as due to the lack of adequate refrigeration facilities and the requirements of the Muslim ritual slaughter, about which the importing countries were very particular.

In the light of the above-mentioned facts, it appears that the process of commercialization of the pastoral sector in Somalia is not a new phenomenon, especially in the northern parts of the country where already in the nineteenth century sales of livestock became quite considerable. In more recent times the South followed suit with an improvement in veterinary services, and above all the opening up of new pastures as a result of well-boring programmes. Increasing commercialization of the pastoral sector must have had an impact on the composition of the herds. The FAO investigation, cited previously, reported a marked shift from reliance on camels and small-stock to cattle, which took place between 1952 and 1964. It is likely that there were also some changes in the sex and age composition. However, no information on such changes is available. The only exception is the data collected in the small coastal district of Merca, situated south of Mogadishu. This information is the result of a multipurpose sample survey undertaken in 1967 in Merca town and a number of villages in the same district. The detailed statistics are limited to cattle only and they indicate that the proportion of males in the total cattle population amounted to 13.7 per cent, while the proportion of bulls of reproductive age expressed as a percentage of the cows of reproductive age was 2.7. Livestock experts suggest that a proportion of 4 per cent is ideal, while 3 per cent is an absolute minimum.[65] No comparable data exists for earlier years. If it could be assumed that similar sex composition has been reached in other parts of the country, the obvious conclusion is that livestock owners went further in their culling practices than is consistent with the normal breeding requirements.

In summary, the statistical data pertaining to pastoral activities in Somalia can only indicate general trends in the crucial variables. Its highly imperfect nature does not permit us to make any definite statements with regard to their year-to-year changes. Thus, we cannot assess with any degree of precision the variations, over time, in the rate of the off-take and its adequacy in terms of the acceptable standards of range management. Also, it is not possible to measure accurately the effects of the progress made in the field of the commercialization of the pastoral sector. We do not know, for certain, to what extent the increased sales of livestock reflected the acceleration in the natural growth of herds, or in what measure they were the result of a weaker tendency to accumulate animals.

The paucity of statistical information has been a major drawback to the Somali planners and the evidence they had to use in order to formulate their policies was much more of a qualitative rather than quantitative nature. It is this factor which is, to a large extent, responsible for the deficiencies in the Somali development planning. It is also this kind of evidence, as it will be shown later on, which leads to the conclusion that the rate of the off-take has not been consistent with the maximum sustainable yield stocking density.

The next section will examine the role played in the development of pastoralism by economic planning.

The colonial development plans, in the former British

Somaliland Protectorate, and the programmes framed under the regime of the U.N. Trusteeship of Somalia, were succeeded by a series of development plans prepared and implemented since independence.

Development Planning and the Nomads

Since the date of Somali independence four development plans have been launched. The first of them covered the years 1963–1967. Its aim, with regard to the livestock sector of the economy, was to increase its output by removing the obstacles to increased production and by creating an additional productive capacity.

In order to achieve these aims, some of the measures proposed an improvement in animal health through better veterinary services and an increase in water supply to open up new grazing lands. These measures, which were of a technical nature, were to be combined with efforts to provide an efficient marketing organization. It was believed that a reduction in animal mortality would assist in increasing the sense of security of the pastoralists, who would find it to their advantage to sell the entire marketable surplus. This, in turn, would lessen the pressure on grazing land which would thus be available for increased production of livestock. As a result of these measures real incomes of the pastoralists would rise together with the exports of livestock which, at the same time, would ameliorate the balance of payments position of the country.[66]

With regard to marketing the Plan relied on the expected results of the transportation and communication programme. Marketing would be assisted by the provision of watering places on routes which were used for the movement of livestock on the hoof, and the establishment of animal collecting centres, meat packing factories and abattoirs.

It was estimated in the Plan that these measures would bring about an increase in livestock production of about 25 per cent during the five-year period. Long-term measures, far exceeding the original planning period, were to include research on animal breeding, introduction of improved breeds, improvement of grazing areas, and the introduction of fodder crops in irrigated areas for fattening the livestock destined for export.[67]

The development strategy applied to the pastoral sector envisaged also the settlement of nomads in ranges especially created in selected areas. These projects would require previous instruction in range management, controlled grazing, provision of fodder and its conservation for dry seasons. Furthermore, improved methods of livestock breeding and animal husbandry and the processing of milk were planned, as well as dry farming in suitable areas to meet the subsistence needs of pastoralists.

It was then realized that a change in the attitudes towards livestock raising would be required for the successful implementation of this part of the programme. The sedentarization of nomads on the irrigated agricultural land was also envisaged, but its purpose was primarily an increase in the production of agricultural crops rather than a long-term solution of over-population in the pastoral sector.

Funds allocated in the Plan to animal husbandry amounted to So.Sh. 14 million, or only one per cent of the total Plan expenditure, and 5.6 per cent of So.Sh. 250 million devoted to agriculture as a whole.[68] These sums were deemed the most essential part of the developmental effort within the pastoral sector. Prior to 1966 no significant action had been taken towards the development of animal husbandry, apart from some reorganization of the veterinary services. By the end of 1964 the amount expended was barely So.Sh. 1.2 million i.e. a fraction of what had been originally planned.[69] In 1966 a major step forward was made by the establishment of the Livestock Development Agency (LDA), a central and autonomous organization. The LDA was made responsible for the development of practically all the major aspects of animal husbandry and the organization and promotion of trade in livestock and livestock products. Most important from the point of view of planning, was the fact that the LDA was made responsible for the coordination of all livestock development programmes and projects.

The overall performance of the first Development Plan fell far short of its targets. Many projects were never implemented and most of those that were carried out did not have the desired effect. The Plan proved too ambitious in terms of the available financial resources, expertise, and the administrative machinery of the government. Consequently, the principal objective of the Short Term Development Programme 1968–1970 was the completion of some of the on-going projects and the creation of basic conditions necessary for the formulation and the implementation of future development plans.[70] The priority was given to the basic infrastructural projects, including transportation, posts and telecommunications and water supplies, to which 70.5 per cent of the total planned expenditure of So.Sh. 705 million was allocated. Funds to be expended on animal husbandry amounted to nearly So.Sh. 46 million, or 6.5 per cent of the total, which was a marked improvement in comparison to the planned expenditure of So.Sh. 14 million during the previous planning period.[71] The Programme reiterated the emphasis on animal disease control and the creation of an efficient marketing system. It also provided for a new pilot project sponsored and financed by the European Economic Community. The project, located in the southern part of Somalia and covering an area of 60,000 square kilometres, was to concentrate on livestock development through a concerted effort in the areas of basic infrastructure, veterinary services, quarantine stations and holding grounds for animals destined for export. The funds to be spent on the EEC Pilot Project during the period 1968–1970 totalled So.Sh. 10 million. By the end of 1969, the estimated total expenditure on animal husbandry reached a figure of So.Sh. 11.3 million, as compared with the originally planned amount of So.Sh. 46 million.

The Third Development Programme 1971–1973 was introduced by the new government which has been in power since the coup of October 1969. It reflected the revolutionary ideology and relied on a socialist approach to development planning. The activities to which priority had been accorded were: livestock, settled agriculture, fisheries, water resources, agro-industries, mineral exploration, training and research, as well as the basic infrastructure. The order of priority was established on the basis of the following four criteria: (1) immediate prospects for substantial returns; (2) opportunities for increased employment; (3) proportion of total population affected by the projects; and (4) prospects of a general and beneficial impact on the economy as a whole.

It can be seen then that the livestock sector, largely neglected in the previous plans, has been raised to its rightful place as it provides livelihood to the bulk of the population and has become an important source of foreign exchange.

Nevertheless, in financial terms, the proportion of development funds allocated to animal husbandry did not reflect the position of first priority. During the years 1971–1973 the outlay on livestock was to reach only 5.9 per cent of the total planned expenditure of So.Sh. 999.9 million, compared to the former allocation of 6.5 per cent. In absolute terms the increase amounted to So.Sh. 13 million, at current prices.[73] The inadequacy of the allotted funds is underscored by the shortcomings in the implementation of the previous Plan. Most of the expenditure over the new planning period was to be devoted to the projects that were not completed, or even those that had never been started. Moreover, many projects included in the Short Term Development Programme 1968–1970 were projects of a continuing nature. It has to be admitted that long-range development of the livestock industry, including the sedentarization of the nomads and the development of livestock raising by the farmers, involved a number of projects outside the strictly defined area of expenditure on animal husbandry. In particular, the supporting projects for livestock development included in other sectors consisted of projects for water resources development implemented by the Ministry of Public Works, as well as the development of 'self-help' water resources and rural roads projects.

The areas of concentration of the Development Programme 1971–1973, followed the pattern of its predecessors, viz., animal disease control, improvement of productivity, and marketing.[74]

The current Plan, covering the years 1974–1978, envisages a total investment of So.Sh. 3,863 million of which 4.2 per cent, or So.Sh. 162 million is to be spent on animal husbandry projects.[75] In absolute terms, the average annual planned expenditure has been increased from nearly So.Sh. 20 million to So.Sh. 32 million. However, an allowance has to be made for the rate of inflation. There is no adequate price index in Somalia, which could be used to assess the fall in the purchasing power of the shilling due to internal inflation,[76] nor are there any published data to estimate the rise in prices of the imported constituents of development projects. It can be presumed, however, that the planned expenditure figures covering the years 1974–1978 have made an allowance for price increases projected on the basis of undisclosed information.

The distribution of outlays among projects shows that nearly one half of the total will be spent on a new Trans-Juba Livestock Development Project; about equal amounts, close to 15 per cent each, will be invested in animal health and ranches and farms projects; over 14 per cent in marketing improvements; and the remaining 6 per cent will be shared by hides and skins improvement projects and artificial insemination centres.[77] It appears that the livestock programme is dominated by a new project aimed at increasing Somalia's meat exports from the area between the Juba River and the Kenya border. Attention was drawn to the potential of this area in the FAO Livestock Development Survey of 1966, which described it as a 'great cattle country'.[78] It is a complex project, whose components include nearly all the elements of the national husbandry programme such as marketing, production ranches, disease control, training of experts, etc.[79]

The new Development Programme restated the long term objectives enunciated in the previous three plans by emphasizing livestock development through a qualitative approach, as distinguished from the purely quantitative changes attempted during the implementation of the earlier programmes. Special attention is paid to the finishing and fattening of cattle, to selection and cross-breeding to improve the potentialities for meat, milk, and wool production, and to the extension of modern technology to the pastoralists. Qualitative improvements are expected to result in the increased rate of off-take from the national herd both for export and local consumption. Ways will also be sought of increasing the returns from export of livestock and livestock products.[80]

The first two Development Plans concentrated on the problems of improvement of animal health, the provision of watering facilities, and the organization of livestock marketing. The emphasis on these aspects led to the neglect of the condition of the range. In the third Development Programme, 1971–1973, the growing awareness of the importance of renewable natural resources became evident. In 1966 a survey of the ecological potentialities of the ranges in the Northern Regions was carried out as part of the programme of range development and management. It was found that the ranges of the North-Western and North-Eastern Regions were in a critical condition. There were several reasons for this state of affairs. Firstly, there had been a sizeable increase in livestock numbers over the previous few years. Secondly, the spread of urban areas and village settlements, and enclosures for private grazing, tended to reduce pastoral movements. Finally, the growth of the port of Berbera, as the major export outlet for livestock, led to the destruction of grasslands in the hinterland which were crossed by numerous stock routes. The conclusion was that a severe drought in the area could be fatal to a large number of animals.

The ranges of Majertinia were not as heavily used as those in the previously discussed areas because the low rainfall makes them less attractive for pastoral nomads. The ranges of Mudugh and those parts of Hiran and Benadir which are situated north of the Shebelle River were in a better condition than those in the Northern Regions. The general impression of the experts was that these ranges represented one of the finest, but the least studied, pastoral lands of the country.[81]

The pastures between the Shebelle and the Juba Rivers were a subject of detailed study carried out by the Agricultural and Water Surveys of 1966.[82] It was found that, owing to the lack of proper range management, the region was deteriorating and its potentialities were far from being fully utilized. The pastoral lands of the inter-river region are located in an area of transition from nomadism to semi-nomadism and sedentary farming and, therefore, they present the problem of integrating animal husbandry with developing agriculture which has a high crop potential. The lands along the two rivers have considerable potentialities but they are seldom used by pastoralists because of the tsetse fly infestation.

Pasture improvement is not practised in Somalia, although experimental work has demonstrated the feasibility of controlled grazing and the provision of forage for the dry seasons by the mowing of natural range. It appears that with adequate range management, large areas of the country could obtain considerable forage reserve capacity representing a potential for future increase in livestock population.[83]

The efforts of successive governments, which go back to the pre-independence period, have been particularly effective in creating the conditions for a rapid growth in livestock numbers. It was the sinking of boreholes and the extension of veterinary services that played a major role in stimulating that trend. But these forms of intervention in the pastoral sector were contributing to a widening gap between the supply of forage offered by the ranges and the demand for it. The situation was made worse by the heavy concentration of pastoral activity in some areas, putting too great a strain on the limited natural resources. The approach of the planners was too one-sided to be beneficial in the long run. Prior to the introduction of the Five Year Development Programme 1974–78, no serious effort was made to improve the rate of off-take from the national herd, and no adequate measures were devised to achieve this aim.

In all fairness to the planners it has to be admitted that in the absence of reliable data on the livestock population and the local meat consumption, the optimal off-take rate cannot be calculated with any degree of precision. The only guideline for livestock policy is the degree of overgrazing. But apart from the influence of controllable variables this criterion is decisively affected by the exogenous stochastic year-to-year variations in the rainfall. The intensification of livestock exports was largely a spontaneous phenomenon, which occurred in the absence of any significant improvement of marketing services by the government agencies responsible for the implementation of development programmes. Nevertheless, the rapid growth of livestock trade did not prove sufficient to raise the off-take rate to an adequate level. The most dramatic increase in the sales of livestock for export took place in the Northern Regions, yet the FAO report of 1967 was emphatic that it was precisely in these areas that a dangerous degree of overstocking has been reached. These views were shared by K. Curry-Lindahl, who visited the area in 1972, during his mission to Somalia.[84]

Matters were made more difficult by the fact that the stockowners were barely eking out a living in these areas of rapidly diminishing returns. No effort to effect destocking was possible without endangering the livelihood of the pastoral community. The solution of the problem depended on the provision of alternative means of support for a considerable proportion of the people.[85]

The Five Year Development Programme 1974–1978 stressed the need for an increase in the rate of off-take, and it reiterated the previous plan's insistence on the improvement in the structure of marketing of livestock as a means for the realization of that objective. Unable to influence directly the pastoralist's tendency to maintain large herds to protect himself against the ravages of animal disease and famine caused by droughts, the government relied on indirect methods. It seems that the force of traditional pastoral attitudes was weakened because of the effect of the disease prevention measures and of the impact of greater availability of water on animal mortality. It was felt that the pastoralist's willingness to sell his livestock could be further increased by way of economic incentives created by better and cheaper marketing arrangements and also by gaining access to new foreign markets where higher prices could be realized.

In the absence of government intervention during the 1960s, marketing has been developed by private initiative into a sophisticated business, which is indicated by the magnitude of the annual export transactions. For example, in 1966 no less than 1,098,000 sheep and goats, 39,000 head of cattle, and 24,000 camels were exported.[86] The buyers of livestock availed themselves of a highly developed credit system operated from the banks, which used as security the letters of credit opened by overseas importers.[87] The first stage of the local organization of marketing relies on purchases from either the pastoralists themselves, who bring in animals to the towns for sale, or by buyers employed by the livestock merchants. The animals are selected according to their quality, the best being destined for export, and the inferior ones sold for local consumption and to the meat canning plants. It has been reported that in the early 1970s livestock trading activity was stimulated as a result of the nationalization of trade in a number of commodities. At that time the interest of many private traders moved to the livestock trade.[88] This would imply a fairly high degree of competition, but a mitigating influence could still be found in the fact that commercial activities in Somalia are affected by lineage affiliations. I. M. Lewis has stressed the importance of the monopolistic-like rights in trade, which had been largely practised in Northern Somaliland along the lines of lineage divisions.[89] The extension of corporate lineage interests into the sphere of livestock trade is probably characteristic of other parts of Somalia today, just as it was true of its Northern Regions.

The FAO Livestock Development Survey of 1966 suggested some far-reaching improvements in the marketing arrangements.

It advocated the creation of holding grounds and quarantine grounds for animals destined for export, improvement in the services provided by municipal markets, the introduction of a minimum price to be paid for cattle delivered to the meat factories, and the lifting of the ban on export of female stock. The long-standing ban on the female stock is the result of a fear that attempts may be made to raise the Somali types of sheep and goats in the Arabian peninsula. Experts were inclined to rule out this possibility. There is no evidence that such attempts were ever made during the long history of Somali livestock exports to Arabia. Furthermore, should the Arab States ever wish to acquire the breeding stock of Somali-type sheep and goats, they could easily import them from the East African territories or from Ethiopia.[90] During the early 1970s the ban was still in existence creating serious obstacles to the increase in the off-take rate that could be realized through the incentive of rising export prices. Other obstacles are presented by factors that could only be overcome over a number of years after the adoption of improved livestock management methods. They include low fertility, high mortality, and the slowness of the physical growth of animals. This last characteristic is of particular importance as the majority of the livestock destined for the market is moved on the hoof. Long distances can only be covered by mature and strong animals. If the concomitant loss of weight is taken into account the provision of adequate road transport is of great importance. It is one of the reasons why expenditure on transport and communications took a prominent place in the Somali development plans.

By 1969, the Livestock Development Agency, established three years earlier, had made some progress in the creation of holding grounds in Berbera and Kismayo, and in addition to the existing livestock market in Mogadishu, a second market was created at the Kismayo holding ground. Greater attention was also paid to the conditions on the cargo vessels carrying animals to the Arabian Peninsula and animal losses en route were considerably reduced.[92] However, the most important recommendations of the FAO Report of 1966 were mostly disregarded. It was discovered that limits of livestock production by extensive grazing were nearly reached. Further expansion required controlled grazing and selective stock management. But the traditional approach of the Somali nomads to pastoralism made the introduction of any new measures, based on the above recommendations, extremely difficult. The age-old custom of treating the range as a common property resource precluded its controlled use.

There is little doubt that the Government's failure to gain popular support for deferred grazing schemes and the creation of famine reserves has contributed, in no small measure, to the precariousness of conditions in the pastoral sector, which was fully revealed by the disastrous drought which struck Somalia in 1974, after nearly three years of failing rainfall. It was an extension of the drought which affected the Sahel and Ethiopia.

The most affected areas of Somalia were the northern ranges. During the last few decades they had been subjected to progressive deterioration due to overpopulation and overgrazing. Apart from the already discussed intervention in the form of badly distributed increases in water supply and veterinary services, little was done to control livestock numbers and to improve the rangeland. It was only during the Short Term Development Programme 1968–1970 that the grazing reserves projects were initiated. The situation was exacerbated by the influx of thousands of nomads from the Ogaden, where they had been affected earlier by the Ethiopian famine. Once the conditions became critical, the Government introduced general price controls, appealed to the public to exercise self-restraint and to volunteer assistance, but above all it organized large-scale relief measures from its own resources and from drought aid granted by a number of foreign countries.[93]

At the beginning of 1975, the Somali Government revealed that approximately 800,000 people (or 25 per cent of the total population) required assistance, and that the immediate relief costs reached US$130 million.[94] The human death toll, attributable directly to the drought, was about 1,500 persons, but livestock losses were estimated to be 80 per cent of cattle, 40 per cent of camels, and 60 per cent of sheep and goats in the affected regions.

By April 1975, the population of the twenty relief camps reached a peak figure of 250,000, and the total number of persons fed by the Government was 700,000. A month later their number rose to 975,000. They were on relief until the end of September, when a bumper harvest, after plentiful spring rains, reduced considerably the number of those in need of assistance. Meanwhile, during the first half of 1975, the Government drew up a rehabilitation plan to resettle 168,000 persons who had lost their livestock and were unable to resume pastoral life. No time was lost to prepare projects to settle 90,000 people on farms in the south of the country, and to employ the remaining 78,000 in fishery projects.[95] By the end of August, after a short period of preparation and training, the prospective farmers were transferred to the areas along the Shebelle and Juba rivers to participate in farming co-operatives. The others were to be settled along the coast to become fishermen.[96] The future fate of these courageous schemes will depend on many factors which are beyond the control of the settlers themselves, and their success will open the road for the government towards an effective solution to the problem of overpopulation in the pastoral sector. Examples of successful drought-induced settlements elsewhere indicate that the reluctance of pastoral nomads to take to farming can be overcome.[97]

Droughts of the magnitude experienced by Somalia in 1974 have not been recorded in the modern history of that country. An explanation of this fact is not difficult to find. Never before were the affected regions exposed to such a degree of overpopulation, both human and animal, as took place there in recent years. Never before were the grasslands more degraded. It is not surprising, therefore, that under these extremely precarious conditions, the failure of rainfall for several consecutive years produced disastrous results.

It is clear that every effort should now be made to prevent their future repetition, the more so as a drought of similar magnitude is certain to set in motion a progressive process of large-scale desertification.

The recent disaster, accompanied by heavy material losses and enormous human suffering, serves as a warning, and it affords a unique opportunity for vigorous action to restore the northern ranges to their normal state.

If, instead, short-term considerations become dominant, and premature efforts are made to restore livestock numbers to the pre-drought level, the tragic end result will not be slow in coming.

NOTES

1. Independent Somalia came to life on 1st July, 1960, as a result of the unification of British Somalia (176,000 square kilometres) and the former Italian Somalia (462,000 square kilometres). Between 1950 and 1960 the latter had been administered by Italy under the U.N. Trusteeship Agreement.

2. 'Gu' and 'Der' are Somali words for the two wet seasons. They are interspersed with the dry seasons 'Hagai' and 'Gilal'.

3. *Inter-River Economic Exploration: The Somali Republic*. U.S. International Cooperation Administration, Washington, D.C., 1961.

4. Somali Republic, *Short Term Development Programme 1968–1970*. Mogadishu, 1968; 58.

5. *Inter-River Economic Exploration*; xii.

6. Somali Republic, *First Five Year Plan 1963–1967*; 1, and Somali Democratic Republic, *Five Year Development Programme 1974–1978*; 8.

7. The first such census was carried in February 1975, but at the time of writing the results were not yet available.

8. Somali Republic, *Statistical Abstract for Somalia*, no. 1, 1964; 1–6.

9. M. Karp, *The Economics of Trusteeship in Somalia*. Boston: Boston University Press, 1960; 27.

10. *Somaliland Report for the years 1958 and 1959*, HMSO, 1960; 11.

11. *Ibid*.

12. Somali Republic, *Multi-purpose Statistical Surveys of Zeila, Hargeisa, Las Anod, Gabileh, Borama, and Erigavo*. Mogadishu 1964.

13. Little research has been done in Somalia on the nature and causes of fertility differentials. One has, therefore, to resort to analogy. The Sudan, a country with similar environmental conditions, was the location of a study which throws some light on the demography of the nomadic communities. According to the results obtained there the fertility differential between nomadic and settled populations was primarily attributable to the fact that a much larger proportion of nomadic women were childless. Moreover, those who had children had tended to start childbearing at a later age and to finish it earlier. They also had longer intervals between the births. In so far as the specific causes are concerned, it appears that health factors were more important than marriage factors. With regard to the former, it was found that nomadic women had experienced appreciably higher rates of pregnancy loss resulting largely from their exacting mode of life; there was also a high incidence of disease. In addition to this they tended to breast-feed for periods of two to three times longer than women in settled communities. The marriage factors responsible for lower fertility included a larger proportion of single women, later average age of marriage, more broken marriages, and more women married to polygamous husbands. Factors were sometimes inter-related, e.g. sterility being often the cause of the divorce or of polygamy (R. A. Henin, 'The Patterns and Causes of Fertility Differentials in the Sudan,' *Population Studies*, vol. 23, 1969).

14. Somali Republic, *Short Term Development Programme 1968–1970*. Mogadishu, 1968; 143.

15. S. B. L. Nigham, *The Manpower Situation in Somalia*. Ministry of Health and Labour, Mogadishu 1965; 11.

16. So far as the late 1960s are concerned this assumption finds partial confirmation in the results of surveys of the thirteen districts in the Southern Region, carried out between 1967 and 1969. They disclosed an average rate of population growth of 2.06 per cent per annum (Somali Democratic Republic, *Statistical Abstract*, 1972; 18).

17. The rate of 2.5 per cent has been applied to the period 1965–1972, in the *World Bank Atlas*, 1974; 6.

18. U.N. Economic Commission for Africa, *Survey of Economic Conditions in Africa*, 1973 (Part I), New York 1974; 19, 26.

19. *Ibid.*, 23.

20. For the method of calculation of animal units see note 20 in ch. 1.

21. J. A. Hunt, *A general survey of the Somaliland Protectorate 1944–1950*. Government of Somaliland Protectorate, London 1951.

22. Somaliland Protectorate, *Report for the years 1956 and 1957*; 19.

23. In 1925 Italy acquired Jubaland from Britain. There was also an annexation of the northern Sultanates. By mid-1928, all of Somalia came under the rule of the colonial government.

24. *Rapport du Gouvernement Italien à l'Assemblée Générale des Nations Unies sur l'administration de Tutelle de la Somalie*, 1954. Rome:Istituto Poligrafico dello Stato, 1955; 255.

25. Somali Republic, *First Five Year Plan 1963–1967*; 42.

26. FAO, *Agricultural and Water Surveys: Somalia; Livestock Development Survey*. Rome 1967; 50.

27. FAO, *loc. cit.*, vol. 1; 12.

28. *Ibid.*, 21.

29. FAO, *loc. cit.*, vol. 4, 117–18.

30. Somali Democratic Republic, *Development Programme 1971–1973*. Mogadishu 1971; 44.

31. P. H. Gulliver, *The Family Herds*. London: Routledge & Kegan Paul, 1955; 244.

32. Cited in R. Pankhurst, 'The Trade of the Gulf of Aden Ports of Africa in the Nineteenth and Early Twentieth Centuries', *Journal of Ethiopian Studies*, vol. 3, 1965; 55.

33. Dressed meat equivalents are assumed to be the same as those used by P. Deane in her work *The Measurement of Colonial National Incomes*. National Institute of Economic and Social Research, Occasional Papers, no. 12; 109.

34. M. Karp, *op. cit.*, 76.

35. *Ibid.*, 77–8.

36. When writing about the Somali herder's well-known reluctance to sell livestock, Karp referred to an article by A. Maugini, 'Lineamenti dell'Economia Rurale della Somalia', *Rivista di Agricoltura Subtropicale e Tropicale*, vol. 47, 1953. Opinions similar to that expressed by Maugini were quite common.

37. R. Pankhurst, *loc. cit.*, 51.
38. *Ibid.*, 53.
39. *Ibid.*, 55–6.
40. *Ibid.*, 40.
41. *Ibid.*, 48.
42. Aden became a British possession in 1839, and after the opening of the Suez Canal in 1869 it developed rapidly.
43. *Ibid.*, 50.
44. *Ibid.*, 36.
45. *Ibid.*, 40, 81.
46. Somaliland Protectorate, *Annual Blue Books 1901–02 to 1938*, passim.
47. Somaliland Protectorate, *Annual Colonial Reports*, passim.
48. This figure is based on 1,814,000 skins exported, 22 kilograms dressed meat equivalent per animal, and approximately 0.5 million people in the Protectorate. The technique of estimating meat consumption on the basis of hides and skins sales, in the absence of other data, has been used elsewhere (see T. J. Aldington and F. A. Wilson, *The Marketing of Beef in Kenya*, Nairobi: The Institute for Development Studies, University College, Occasional Paper no. 3, 1968). The data available did not cover information on the year to year changes in stocks related to price fluctuations, and the numbers of hides and skins used for domestic purposes, as well as the skins of animals whose meat was not consumed. It is superfluous to mention that calculations of this kind are subject to a considerable margin of error.
49. *Annual Blue Books*, passim.
50. M. Guillain, *Documents sur l'histoire, la géographie et le commerce de l'Afrique Orientale*, Deuxième Partie. Paris: Arthus Bertrand, 1850; 486, 508.
51. R. Pankhurst, 'The Trade of Southern and Western Ethiopia and the Indian Ocean Ports in the Nineteenth and Early Twentieth Centuries,' *Journal of Ethiopian Studies*, vol. 3, 1965.
52. *Ibid.*, 53–4.
53. G. Rocchetti, 'Gli scambi commerciali della Somalia,' *Rivista di Agricoltura Subtropicale e Tropicale*, vol. 49, 1955; 281.
54. *Ibid.*, 282.
55. *Ibid.*, 283.
56. Based on data from P. Cozzi, 'L'allevamento del bestiame in Somalia', *Rivista di Agricoltura Subtropicale e Tropicale*, vol. 59, 1965; 135, and Ministère des Affaires Etrangeres: *Rapport du Gouvernement Italien à l'Assemblée Générale des Nations Unies sur l'Administration de Tutelle de la Somalie 1959*. Rome 1960; 234–57.
57. Based on data from *Annual Colonial Reports*. The comparisons between the physical quantities exported from the two territories are frustrated by the nature of the original time series which are expressed in quintals in the one case and numbers of animals in the other.
58. Somali Republic, *Statistical Abstracts*; passim.
59. Somali Republic, *Foreign Trade Returns*, 1966.
60. Repubblica Italiana, Ministero degli Affari Esteri, *L'Amministrazione*

Fiduciaria della Somalia e i Rapporti dell' Italia con la Repubblica Somalia. Rome 1961; 68. P. Cozzi, *loc. cit.*, 127.

61. Until 1965 foreign trade returns were shown separately for the Southern and Northern Regions. As from 1966 statistics reflect complete uniformity of the system and do not distinguish any more between the two parts of the country.
62. P. Cozzi, *loc. cit.*, 136.
63. The possible impact of other factors cannot be dismissed, particularly better utilization of the existing stocks.
64. The Banana Monopoly (Azienda Monopolio Banane) ceased to exist in 1964.
65. Somali Republic, *Statistical Abstract*, 1967; 49.
66. Somali Republic, *First Five Year Plan 1963–1967*; 42.
67. *Ibid.*, 43.
68. *Ibid.*, 37, 46.
69. *Somali National Bank Bulletin No. 4*, 1965; 30–33.
70. Somali Republic, *Short Term Development Programme 1968–1970*; 1–3.
71. *Ibid.*, 4.
72. Somali Democratic Republic, *Development Programme 1971–1973*; 6–8.
73. *Ibid.*, 177.
74. *Ibid.*, 56–9.
75. Somali Democratic Republic, *Five Year Development Programme 1974–1978*; 27.
76. There is no price index for the country as a whole and the Cost of Living Index for Mogadishu, published since 1950, is not representative of price changes in the rest of the country.
77. Somali Democratic Republic, *loc. cit.*, 73–4.
78. FAO, Livestock Development Survey; 14.
79. Somali Democratic Republic, *loc. cit.*, 54–6.
80. *Ibid.*, 38–9.
81. Somali Democratic Republic, *Development Programme 1971–1973*; 45–6.
82. FAO, *loc. cit.*
83. *Ibid.*, 11–14.
84. K. Curry-Lindahl, 'Conservation Problems and Progress in Equatorial African Countries', *Environmental Conservation*, vol. 1, 1974; 119–20.
85. FAO, *loc. cit.*, 17.
86. Somali Republic, *Statistical Abstract*, 1967; 84.
87. FAO, *loc. cit.*, 29.
88. Somali Democratic Republic, *Five Year Development Programme 1974–1978*; 7.
89. I. M. Lewis, 'Lineage Continuity and Modern Commerce in Northern Somaliland' in *Markets in Africa*, edited by P. Bohannan and G. Dalton, Evanston: Northwestern University Press, 1968; 380.
90. FAO, *loc. cit.*, 30.
91. Personal communication from the former FAO Chief Livestock Adviser.
92. *Ibid.*
93. I. M. Lewis, 'The Drought in Perspective' in *Abaar, The Somali Drought*, edited by I. M. Lewis, London: International African Institute, 1975; 2–3.

94. Information disclosed by the Economic Adviser to the Somali Government, Ibrahim Megag Samantar, during a press conference held on 29th January 1975, in the United States (*Abaar*, 34).

95. The Economist Intelligence Unit, *Quarterly Economic Review of Uganda, Ethiopia, Somalia*, 2nd Quarter, 1975; 10.

96. *Ibid.*, 3rd Quarter, 1975; 14. According to a later report the number of displaced nomads who were moved to fishing villages was around 15,000 (*Barclays Country Reports: Somalia*, Oct. 3, 1977).

97. One such recent example is described by Ben Wisner (*Abaar*, 24–5).

Chapter Five

THE SAHELIAN DROUGHT

Introduction

The recent calamity which struck the Somali pastoralists has been overshadowed by events in the Sahel (see Map 2, p 9), both in terms of the size of the area, the numbers of people and animals affected, and in the extent of publicity accorded to them. The Sahelian drought also became a topic of several conferences, symposia and scientific reports.[1]

The present chapter concentrates on a comparison and critical assessment of the views on the Sahelian drought expressed in two important publications dealing with this subject. These include 'The Sahelian Drought and its Demographic Implications' by John C. Caldwell (1975), and 'A Systems Analysis of Pastoralism in the West African Sahel' by Anthony C. Picardi (1974).

The six countries of the Sahel-Sudan region (Mauritania, Senegal, Mali, Upper Volta, Niger, Chad) cover an area of 5.3 million square kilometres – slightly more than one-half the size of Canada – and their mid-1972 population of 24.1 million was nearly 10 per cent higher than Canada's population. Four of the six countries (Mali, Upper Volta, Niger, and Chad) were included in the United Nations list of the twenty-five least developed economies of the world. The chief characteristics of these countries, which have a major bearing upon the economic development of the region, include a chronic susceptibility to ecological destruction, an absence of human development and the lack of an indigenous skilled and professional labour force, as well as a poor natural resource endowment. Moreover, the sparsity of population has contributed to unusually high costs of government services and has thwarted the development of an infrastructure.

The socio-economic policies that have been followed in the past have been unfavourable to the majority of the people living in the traditional sector.

The region's pattern of economic development has created an unusually high degree of dependence on foreign aid. But in the absence of the necessary local ingredients the effectiveness of this high level of foreign assistance has been very small.[2]

There are a number of major differences in human and resource endowments as well as in the economic performance of the countries of the Sahel-Sudan region. Reliance on cash crops and minerals is the exception rather than the rule. The economy of Senegal relies on groundnuts – its most important crop – while Mauritania exploits rich iron ore deposits. Recently Niger became an important producer of uranium.[3]

In 1972, the per capita incomes of Senegal and Mauritania were $260 and $180 respectively. The per capita incomes of the remaining four countries, which had nothing comparable to either Senegal's groundnuts, or Mauritania's iron, ranged between $70 for Upper Volta and $90 for Niger.[4] Senegal has outdistanced the remaining economies of the Sahel in the fields of industrialization and urbanization. In 1970 the share of Senegal's industrial sector in its GDP amounted to 16 per cent, and nearly one-third of its population were town dwellers. The corresponding figures in the other five countries ranged between 2 and 10 per cent and 5 and 12 per cent respectively.

The 1971 per capita values of exports for Mauritania and Senegal, the only two countries of the region which have access to the sea, were $75 and $31, while these values ranged from only $3 to $9 for the rest. Similarly, the per capita value of imports, in the same year, ranged from $54 for Senegal down to $9 for Upper Volta.[5]

In spite of the above differences the countries of the Sahel-Sudan region share a number of fundamental problems which are created by environmental, and human resources constraints, and a number of factors of a socio-economic nature.

Between the years 1969 and 1973, the drought had its major impact on an area extending from the coast of Mauritania to Western Sudan. It is known as the Sahel and it covers over one-quarter of the area of the six countries of the region. The Sahel stretches north of the 15°N., and its climate is arid and semi-arid, with an average annual rainfall of less than 600 mm, concentrated in the months of June to August. The vegetation consists chiefly of steppe grasslands and degraded shrub. Because of the nature of the environment the dominant form of economic activity in the Sahel is pastoral nomadism, while in the Sudanic zone, extending to the south (between 10° and 15°N.), it is that of the shifting cultivation of millet and sorghum. The natural division between the two belts is determined by the tsetse fly. Its presence south of about 14°N. explains why mixed farming is not practised, except in the transitional area.[6] Different patterns of economic activity in the two belts stimulate economic relations between their inhabitants and promote the exchange of pastoral products for cereals and other goods provided by the South.

Between 1969 and 1973, low rainfall affected nearly eight million square kilometres, while the region of acute distress totalled approximately 2.5 million square kilometres. Apart from the Ethiopian provinces of Wollo and Tigre, and northern parts of Somalia, nearly all this region lies in West Africa.[7]

The analyses discussed below pay attention to a number of aspects of the Sahelian drought. The first of them emphasizes the importance of the human population growth.

The Drought and Demography

John C. Caldwell, Professor of the Australian National University, is one of the leading authorities on demographic problems in Africa, and was an eyewitness to the 1973 events in the Sahel. He assessed the losses in livestock and human populations in the Sahel but he admits that the nature of evidence made him very cautious. The public has been misled by numerous journalistic reports which were of a rather sensational nature. The official sources of information were equally unreliable and the disparities between their estimates were astronomical. The August 1973 Report to the President of the United States on the Sahelian Drought claimed a 50 per cent

death rate among animals, AID estimates were under 40 per
cent,[8] FAO calculated a 25 per cent loss of cattle in 1973, and
French Development Aid reported losses of over 20 per cent.[9]

Caldwell doubts whether reliable estimates of the percentage of
animals lost were possible as there were no long-term studies of
animal numbers. Existing estimates depended on cattle tax
figures, which probably understated numbers.[10] Accurate
estimates of losses could not be made because a large proportion
of the animals were moved south, and while some died on the
way, others were sold. Also calving rates decreased sharply, as
they always do in a drought situation, and consequently the total
number fell proportionately. Last but not least, fluctuations in
animal numbers are a normal phenomenon, and it was not quite
logical to measure losses in terms of a reduction in the numbers
previously inflated as a result of a particularly good period.[11]

Reports on human losses were equally distorted. The Report to
the President of the United States of August 1973 put the deaths
attributable to the drought at one hundred thousand.[12] Caldwell
suspects that this figure can be traced back to an estimate
published by the Centre for Disease Control in Upper Volta
which, in view of some unreasonably high estimates of deaths in
Mauritania, Mali, Niger, and Upper Volta, assessed the
theoretical limit of mortality due to famine based upon the most
extreme data obtained. The estimate amounted to 101,000 deaths
and was related to a population of about 2.2 million nomads in
the four countries. Death rates of the sedentary population were
reported to have been the same as in the previous years.[13]

What conclusion does Caldwell draw about the increase in
human mortality arising from the drought of the early 1970s?
Press reports were often little more than mere figments of the
imagination. The same was true of the many apparently reliable
statements. The statistical systems did not meet the challenge.
Undoubtedly, death rates must have gone up, especially among
nomads, but not on the scale suggested by the drought publicity.
People proved to have a surprising capacity for survival. They ate
the plants known to have food value, which were rarely
consumed in good years; they killed game and domestic animals,
and moved south to safer places. Human losses were also
prevented by foreign aid, which was provided in large
quantities.[14]

To sum up, in the absence of reliable demographic data, only the most general impressions can be formed about the effect of the recent drought on the size and composition of the population. Moreover, very little is known about the magnitude of migration, which was an important factor in the drive for survival.

Important contributory factors to the tragic situation in which the Sahelian nomads found themselves during the years 1970–74 can be traced to human intervention that led to disregard of the fragile nature of the local ecology. The control of disease by vaccination and immunization had permitted the animal population to increase rapidly. Watering facilities for animals had been considerably extended through the well-boring programmes, but at the same time nothing had been done to improve the grasslands which the enlarged herds destroyed – especially was this true of the pastures around waterholes. Consecutive good seasons together with improved watering facilities encouraged the nomads to intensify their movements further to the north where the conditions of the environment were increasingly precarious.[15] The tragedy of the Sahel is the best example of a crisis which was triggered off by good intentions that turned into a disaster.

Caldwell warns that the nomadic way of life is imperilled by the growth of the nomadic population. Even now an improvement in living standards of this group can probably be achieved only by reducing their numbers. The nomad population in the Sahel is estimated at 2.5 million, with a growth rate of 1.5 per cent per annum.[16] If the present demographic trends continue – and Caldwell does not envisage any rapid changes in the crude birth and death rates – their number would double within forty-six years. This, however, should not be permitted to happen. His projections, which take account of his own population policy recommendations, assume a stable nomadic population.

How can this be achieved? National planners suggest that enforced sedentarization may be the only way of solving the problem.[17] The merits of such an once-and-for-all solution are questionable. Northern grasslands are a national asset for which no alternative uses exist, apart from livestock herding. A complete removal of pastoral nomads from these areas will amount to a net economic loss for the society as a whole, unless it can be prevented by the substitution of commercial ranching.

It is a well-known fact that nomads cannot easily be turned into farmers because of their cultural resistance. It is easier for them to settle down to urban occupations. This has been the experience in Mauritania and in a number of North African countries. The recent drought may well stimulate a type of population movement that increasingly seems inevitable: organized resettlement schemes.[18] With the assistance of this approach the nomadic population may be reduced to a desired size, or it may be prevented from growing above its present level.

The M.I.T. Report

The set of recommendations outlining the strategies for the development of the Sahel-Sudan Region contained in the report, which henceforth we shall call the M.I.T. Report,[19] represents a comprehensive approach. The recommendations deal with all the sectors of the six economies of the region and, therefore, go far beyond our sphere of interest. One must not lose sight of the fact that there is a close interaction between the sectors, and the policies affecting them are interrelated. Moreover, an economy if it is to be understood properly should be viewed in the context of the environment in which it works, and this necessitates a systemic approach. Bearing these points in mind, we shall concentrate our attention on a particular part of the M.I.T. Report, viz. its Annex No.5, entitled 'A Systems Analysis of Pastoralism in the West African Sahel' written by A. C. Picardi. It is an in-depth study, confined to an area of ten million hectares (approximately 101,000 square kilometres), situated in the Sahelian part of Niger, north of Tahoua. In 1963, it was inhabited by 100,000 Tuaregs and Fulani, 574,000 head of cattle, 194,000 camels, and 963,000 sheep and goats.[20]

The choice of the area for the purpose of this study was influenced by its characteristics, which are representative of the remaining parts of the Sahel, as well as by the requirements dictated by the application of a computer simulation model, which necessitated a certain minimum of quantitative information. The limited size of the area facilitated the task of obtaining the necessary data.

The purpose of the model was to relate the interactions among the ecosystem, livestock herds and the human population. The essence of the problem dealt with can best be described as 'the tragedy of the commons' – a catchword borrowed from the title of a well-known article by Garrett Hardin, who likened the earth's natural resources to a common pasture on which everyone grazes his livestock.[21] As under a system of the common ownership of the rangeland there is no control over the number of animals each person grazes, the common pasture is inevitably destroyed. Similarly, the sudden collapse of the pastoral system in the Sahel, precipitated by the drought, came concurrently with the increasing destruction of the rangeland.

Computer simulations and historical accounts date chronic overgrazing of the Sahel back to the early 1960s, resulting in progressive desertification.[22] Computer simulations were also to follow up the effects of the technical assistance programmes proposed in 1974 by the Comité Permanent Interétats de Lutte Contre la Sécheresse Dans le Sahel (CILSS), sponsored by the francophone West African states after the recent drought. In addition to the intensification of veterinary services which aimed at a reduction of the death rates of livestock, and well-boring schemes, the programmes included herd breeding and restocking measures to increase herds to their pre-drought levels. The most respectable of all were reforestation and reseeding projects, which would shorten the time required for recovery of rangeland vegetation.[23]

In the previous section we have described the first two of these measures as leading directly to a crisis with positive origins, when intuitive programmes produce counter-intuitive results. There are no reasons to question the good intentions which motivated these programmes, but there are strong grounds for questioning the planners' understanding of the problems they are attempting to solve. Implicit in their approach, based on the intensification of the traditional types of aid, is the erroneous assumption that the vagaries of weather are alone responsible for the tragedy of the Sahel.

A simulation model, developed by Picardi, has shown that these programmes, if implemented, would result in swift and complete desertification of the range, in spite of the optimistic reforestation and reseeding schemes.[24]

In addition to the above scenario, Picardi postulates seven other policy sets introducing various packages of policy methods and intended objectives. It is not within the scope of the present discussion to go into the details of all the remaining simulation models. Nevertheless, some of the conclusions arrived at, on their basis, may be of interest. The first of them is that a system of management aiming at the preservation of the natural resource represented by rangeland is incompatible with the preservation of the traditional decision-making structure. It lacks a strong enough feedback from the range condition to the off-take rate. Secondly, accelerated population growth, resulting from improvements in health, is incompatible with increases in material wealth. The absolute amount of wealth to be shared depends on the carrying capacity of the rangeland, which is limited. For similar reasons, food shortage can be eliminated only when population is stabilized at a level compatible with per capita production consistent with an adequate diet. Continued out-migration has its limits and cannot be relied upon indefinitely.

In Picardi's opinion a successful, though unconventional, approach is to be found in a system under which the pastoralists assign priority to range conservation. This condition has been incorporated in the simulation model with a starting point in 1975. Cooperation on the part of the herders would make it possible to destock the range to the sustainable maximum yield-carrying capacity. In 1980 an additional feeding programme would be introduced. Sales of livestock removed for conservation purposes would assist in covering the cost of the feeding programme. Eventually the simulated economic programme introduces price increases which are effective in protecting the herdsmen against future famines. As a result, their cultural attitudes change, the social importance of animals is greatly reduced and the tendency to maintain livestock as a necessary insurance against adversity disappears. This permits steady improvement in the quality of the soil, a process which can be accomplished over a period of about one hundred years. During the later stages of this scenario marked increase in off-take rates becomes possible because of the growing productive potential and the changing attitudes. Adequate off-take continues to be instrumental in maintaining the sustained yield-carrying capacity. The off-take rates level off at approximately 25 per cent, i.e. about twice the level under traditional management. The upper limit of the system is reached by the year 2030, when both the population growth and the standard of living are stabilized. The existing resource base can support no more people at their desired level of living.[25]

Picardi seems to realize fully that, in reality, the range conservation concept has no room in the traditional value structure of the pastoralists. If destocking cannot be done voluntarily, the solution may have to be found in a system of expensive incentives or costly disincentives. But such costs may appear to be irrational when viewed in the light of other opportunities. Alternatively, strict stock controls may have to be imposed, whose implementation would involve serious practical and ethical issues.[26]

Thus the most efficient way of changing basic pastoral attitudes remains an open question.

Comparison and Assessment of Caldwell's and Picardi's Approaches

The difference between Caldwell's and Picardi's views on what ought to be done in order to solve the problems of the Sahel reflects the disagreement between them on the nature of the recent Sahelian drought and its consequences. The pertinent questions to be answered are, firstly, whether the last drought differed in any significant way from the previous ones? If so, will this imply a basic change in Sahel's economy? Caldwell rejects the hypothesis of a permanent climatic change in West Africa. He questions the view that the 1969–73 drought was the worst ever, but admits that it was the first of its magnitude since the Second World War. Having occurred at a time of growing concern about the world's resources, it received massive publicity. The existing records indicate that in the eighteenth century five-year droughts were not unknown in that part of Africa, and most of the older savannah people believe that the drought of 1911–14 was the worst in living memory. The droughts of the early 1920s and early 1940s appear to have been almost as bad.

According to Caldwell, none of the rainfall series for the West African savannah support a theory of a secular climatic change. The existing pattern seems to be one of short-term fluctuations and it is unlikely that the future Sahelian rainfall pattern will vary greatly from that which has been known for years. Caldwell does not accept the prophets' of doom dictum that the recent drought spelled an irreversible change in the pastoral way of life. In his opinion '... economic and demographic change will continue in the savannah at the kind of modest rate that the environment dictates ...'[27]

While Caldwell concentrates his attention on the irregularities of the weather, Picardi emphasizes the results of human activity over the pasty fifty years and the impact of the pre-drought decade of above-average rainfall. The period of time with exceptionally good pastures combined with exogenous man-made interventions, such as the elimination of warfare, the digging of wells, and the provision of veterinary services, resulted in an unprecedented increase in livestock population and this, in its turn, led to overstocking and progressive desertification. This process must have continued for a long time before it became a generally recognized problem in the middle 1960s. The latest drought has been accompanied by a sudden extension of the desertified area and, therefore, a marked decrease in the productive capacity of the rangeland.[28]

It is mainly for this reason that Picardi views the recent West African drought as significantly different from preceding droughts, even if the actual deficit of annual rainfall was in no sense unique.[29]

Both authors, while concentrating their attention mainly on the recent events in the Sahel, limit themselves in their interpretative efforts to very few facts from the economic history of the region. Their analysis of the present is thus deprived of a background which would make it far more comprehensible.

The scanty historical evidence used by Caldwell and the conclusions he draws from it should not be left without some comment. He is not quite correct in complaining about a lack of regional livestock data for the past decades. He refers to a report which covered a third of a century and dealt mostly with the Bornu area in north-eastern Nigeria.[30] But the French authorities supplied estimates of livestock population for 1947, for French West Africa and the French Equatorial Africa. The original data relied on livestock tax returns, which excluded cattle and camels below three years of age and sheep and goats below one year of age. Nevertheless the introduction of vaccination procedures for young animals during the 1940s permitted them to assess their numbers with a fair degree of accuracy. The final livestock data included all the necessary corrections and were a conservative reflection of the post-war stocks.[31]

A comparison of the livestock numbers, expressed in animal units, between 1947 and the late 1960s shows a nearly twofold increase from 9.3 million to 17.7 million.[32] As most of the stock was concentrated in the Sahel zone, it can be assumed that the magnitude of the increase reflected the situation in that area.

Relying on a case study of the Kanem region of northern Chad, where livestock losses during the drought years attained 44 per cent, and accepting a similar figure for the rest of the Sahel, Caldwell concludes that it is unlikely that the livestock numbers were by 1973 any smaller than they were in the early 1940s or even the late 1940s.[33] His assumption is confirmed by evidence obtained from sources which have not found a place in his report, since a 44 per cent reduction in the pre-drought stock would still leave 0.6 million animal units over and above the 1947 level.

The account given by Caldwell of the factors, other than purely demographic, which have been gradually contributing to the deterioration of the nomads' ability to protect themselves against the vagaries of the climate, is far less convincing. He states that during the droughts nomads could earn their living by participating in the trans-Saharan and intra-Saharan caravans, or could supplement their dwindling resources by raising the level of levies or even attacking the caravans. But, explains Caldwell, by the eighteenth century caravanning was dwindling and the final blows have fallen this century when railways and roads reached the savannah.[34]

The truth is, however, that the trans-Saharan trade increased during the nineteenth century and the final decline did not come till the last quarter.[35] A recent study of the trade of a Sahelian region, which concentrates on the Tripoli-Kano route, moves the date of the final decline to the end of the nineteenth century. After about 1905 the regional trade was redirected to the south. It relied on transactions in grain, cattle, small-stock and pack oxen.[36] Furthermore, the collapse of the trans-Saharan caravan trade in the twentieth century did not destroy the opportunities for the use of animal transport. The latter complemented the modern system of transportation until the 1950s. Adding to factors which contributed to the continuation and the redirection of caravan trade was the rise in the demand for new goods. Meanwhile, the caravans following the traditional routes to the north, particularly those bringing salt from Toadenni, have also been on the increase.[37]

During the first half of the twentieth century motor transport hardly competed with animal transport in such important branches of nomadic commercial activity as the trade in salt and in cereals. Moreover, there was a division of labour: motor transport moved along the main routes and the camels were used on feeder roads and to reach nomadic encampments.[38]

Both Caldwell and Picardi disregard the way in which one of the more recent methods of increasing pastoral resources tended to intensify the impact of the drought by preventing migration to the south. This was the paradox of the boreholes. Before the large-scale well-drilling programmes were introduced in the Sahel, the shortage of water preceded the degradation of grasslands. Drying wells served as a signal to the nomads to start their migration to the south. Deep wells providing a constant water supply acted as a trap to the herders and their animals. The boreholes attracted large numbers of livestock, and the pastures within an increasingly widening radius around them suffered from overgrazing, a situation which was intensified by the drought conditions. The smaller wells dried up and the distances between the boreholes through barren land were too great, cutting off the escape routes for the nomads.[39] This new phenomenon is vitally important in any attempt to account for the difference between the last drought and its predecessors.

Caldwell sees the solution of the Sahel's economic problem in a reduction in human population. His recommendation follows the right direction but does not go far enough. Picardi, in his sophisticated computer model, combines Caldwell's population policy (large-scale out-migration and family planning) with eleven additional programmes and policies.[40]

The efficiency of the solution proposed by Caldwell is precluded by the outcome of Picardi's eight scenarios based on various combinations of the eleven programmes and policies.

In his final effort, Picardi achieves the desired outcome by introducing an additional approach into his 'successful' policy set, in terms of which the herdsmen assign priority to range conservation rather than to their own immediate, individual welfare. He realizes the difficulty of incorporating range preservation concepts in the value structure of the nomads and finds it impossible to inform us how can this task be accomplished. But is it reasonable to expect the Sahelian pastoralists to solve promptly the fundamental problem of their environment? Before an attempt is made to answer this question one should perhaps reflect on our own inability to prevent the 'tragedy of the commons' from being a daily occurrence in our own part of the world.

A Third Point of View

While the results of Picardi's analysis of the Sahelian problem lead to pessimistic conclusions, the conference on 'International Development Strategies for the Sahel' held in 1974 at Bellagio[41] seems to have been permeated by a spirit of cautious optimism. The participants at the conference agreed that development in the Sahel is possible.

According to their views, the vexed problem of obstacles created by traditional pastoral attitudes could be solved if the tribal people were given a strong hand in the planning. They would then adapt to new production systems within fairly wide limits and their involvement would remove the drawbacks of the 'development from above'. Their participation and cooperation could be enhanced by a system of economic incentives.[42]

Ideas were also expressed on the costs of development implied by alternative strategies. Useful guides were provided for the formulation of a more rigorous approach in terms of cost-benefit analyses. First of all, it is imperative to compare the growing costs of assistance necessitated by the recurring droughts with the once-and-for-all cost of reclamation and development.[43] There was little doubt in the minds of the participants that in the long run the periodic emergency schemes would be more costly. For instance stored feeds, such as silage, would be far less expensive and more efficacious than air drops in emergency periods.[44]

Once the idea of reclamation and development is accepted,[45] a choice would have to be made between moving some of the nomads and their livestock to the south, whenever weather conditions require it, and transporting the necessary supplies to the north.[46] As either of these strategies would rely on regional resources and their development, no question of outside emergency assistance would arise.[47]

It was also stressed that the development of the Sahel, if it is to be successful, must be based on a holistic approach involving full cooperation between the States of the region and encompassing the totality of its life, resources, and relationships. The emphasis must change from short-term, project-based national effort to a long-term, regional-based effort.[48]

A proposal designed along these lines has been put forward by one of the participants at the conference, G. M. Van Dyne, who considered the possibility of employing a land use concept embracing the arid, semi-arid, sub-humid, and humid areas of the Sahel and the adjacent sub-regions as a complex, and putting up to 25 per cent of the land in some zones into strategically located multiple-use grazing commons which would assist in relieving the pressure on the northern grasslands during the periods of drought.[49]

The strategy proposed by Van Dyne relies on the integration of livestock grazing in the northern and southern parts of the region; it furthermore relies on the development of transport and the creation of abattoirs in the southern zone, the utilization of intensive irrigated agriculture for food production, and the use of concentrate feeds made from industrial by-products to supplement the needs of livestock in the grazing areas.

The lands in the arid and semi-arid zones would be developed as national grazing reserves to be used primarily under emergency conditions. Also it was suggested that grazing loads should be spread during periods of abundant rainfall in order to maximize the revegetation of specific deteriorated areas.[50] Voluntary joint tribal agreements would be sought for integrated management of the arid and semi-arid rangeland systems and government-controlled grazing reserves further south.[51]

The implementation of a programme relying on the above strategy would require not only a free movement across the national boundaries, but also far-reaching economic cooperation between the States of the Sahel region. Only then unimpeded migration, acting as 'insurance' against drought, could take place. Fattening farms could also be introduced in southern locations, which are unsuitable for breeding operations because of the dangers of trypanosomiasis. These farms, however, would be ideal as an outlet for livestock being culled from Sahelian herds.

Southern economies are likely to intensify the interest in the Sahel's livestock industry, as their demand for animal protein is expanding. This is the case in Senegal, and particularly in Nigeria, where personal incomes are growing rapidly.[52]

In conclusion, the re-establishment of the freedom of nomadic movements within the whole of the Sahel-Sudan area is a necessary condition for the survival and development of the pastoral economy of the region. Its timely fulfilment is far more a matter of political decisions than of economic feasibility. While the role of an economic historian is to unearth the relevant facts of the past, and to show the importance of the links which vitalized the relations between the North and the South, the role of a contemporary politician is to accept the message and to draw appropriate conclusions.

The right step in this direction has already been made in 1976, with the ratification of the treaty establishing the Economic Community of West African States (ECOWAS).[53] The future will show how efficient the cooperation will be between the member States, and whether the time gap in its implementation will not ruin the chances for a timely solution of the problems of the Sahel's imperilled pastoral economy.

NOTES

1. To mention just a few: D. Dalby and R. J. Harrison Church (eds.), *Drought in Africa*, Report of the 1973 Symposium. London: Centre for African Studies, School of Oriental and African Studies, University of London, 1973; *Working Papers: Conference on International Development, Strategies for the Sahel, 1974*. The Rockefeller Foundation, 1975; J. C. Caldwell, *The Sahelian Drought and its Demographic Implications*. American Council on Education, 1975; A. C. Picardi, *A Systems Analysis of Pastoralism in the West African Sahel*. Center for Policy Alternatives, Massachusetts Institute of Technology, 1974.

2. *A Framework for Evaluating Long Term Strategies for the Development of the Sahel-Sudan Region*. Center for Policy Alternatives, Massachusetts Institute of Technology, 1974. Annex 1, Economic Considerations for Long Term Development, 1–5.

3. *Africa Research Bulletin*, December 15, 1975–January 14, 1976, 3752.

4. World Bank Atlas, 1974, 7.

5. *A Framework for Evaluating Long Term Strategies for the Development of the Sahel-Sudan Region*, Annex 1, 5–6.

6.   J. C. Caldwell, *loc. cit.*, 5

7.   *Ibid.*, 3.

8.   Agency for International Development, Department of State, 'Disaster Memo, no. 11: Central/West Africa – Sahelian Zone Drought', mimeographed report, Washington, 6th May 1973; quoted in Caldwell, *loc. cit.*, 20.

9.   FAO., 'Toll of Cattle in Sahelian Zone Topped 3.5 Million' Press Release, 74/5, Rome, 23rd January 1974; quoted in Caldwell, *loc. cit.*, 21.

10.   J. C. Caldwell, *loc. cit.*, 21–2.

11.   The 1960s represented a particularly good period for the pastoralists because of above normal rainfall.

12.   R. H. Faulkingham, et al., 'The demographic effects of drought in the West African Sahel: The Nigerian village of Tudu', Population Association of America, Annual Meeting, New York, April 1974, 3; quoted in Caldwell, *loc. cit.*, 23.

13.   J. C. Caldwell, *loc. cit.*, 24.

14.   *Ibid.*, 26–27.

15.   *Ibid.*, 42.

16.   *Ibid.*, passim.

17.   Most of the Governments of the Sahelian countries are dominated by the sedentary farming element, whose views are, to this day, influenced by an age-old animosity between the rural and nomadic populations.

18.   J. C. Caldwell, *loc.cit.*, 72.

19.   *A Framework for Evaluating Long-Term Strategies for the Development of the Sahel-Sudan Region.*

20.   A. C. Picardi, *op. cit.*, 36–37.

21.   Garrett Hardin, 'The Tragedy of the Commons'. *Science*, vol. 162, 1968, 1243–8.

22.   A. C. Picardi, *op. cit.*, passim.

23.   *Ibid.*, 95–96.

24.   *Ibid.*, 98–103.

25.   *Ibid.*, 174–195. Also A. C. Picardi and W. W. Seifert, 'A Tragedy of the Commons in the Sahel', *Technology Review*, May 1976, 48–51.

26.   A. C. Picardi, 'Practical and ethical issues of development in traditional societies: insights from a system dynamics study in pastoral West Africa', *Simulation*, vol. 26, 1976, 9.

27.   J. C. Caldwell, *loc. cit.*, 19–20, 66.

28.   A. C. Picardi, *op. cit.*, 57–60.

29.   *Ibid.*, 53.

30.   J. C. Caldwell, *loc. cit.*, 21.

31.   Encyclopédie de l'Empire Français, Afrique Occidentale Française, L'Elevage, vol. 1; Paris: Encyclopédie Coloniale et Maritime, 1949; 355–6. Encyclopédie de l'Union Française, Afrique Equatoriale Française, L'Elevage; Paris: Encyclopédie Coloniale et Maritime, 1950, 335.

32.   The livestock data for the late 1960s rely on the information included in *Surveys of African Economies*, vols. 1–6, Washington, D.C.: International Monetary Fund, 1968–1973; and J. Clauzel, 'Evolution de la vie

économique et des structures sociales du pays nomade du Mali de la conquête française à l'autonomie interne', *Tiers Monde*, vol. 3, 1962.

33. J. C. Caldwell, *loc. cit.*, 22.

34. *Ibid.*, 40–41.

35. C. W. Newbury, 'North African and Western Sudan Trade in the Nineteenth Century: A Re-valuation', *Journal of African History*, vol. 7, 1966, 233–46.

36. S. Baier, 'Trans-Saharan Trade and the Sahel: Damergu 1870–1930', *Journal of African History*, vol. 18, 1977, 37–60.

37. J. Clauzel, *loc. cit.*, 295–6.

38. *Ibid.*, 307.

39. S. Baier, 'Economic History and Development: Drought and the Sahelian Economies of Niger', *African Economic History*, vol. 1, 1976, 9.

40. The complete list of programmes and policies includes: direct stock control; supplemental feeding; veterinary measures; herd management; policy to increase material wealth aspirations; price policy; public health programme; nutrition programme; education programme; policy to decrease social importance of cattle; policy to induce herdsmen to assign priority to range conservation; Picardi, *op. cit.*, Table 7.4–2, 178.

41. *Working Papers, The Rockefeller Foundation Conference in International Development Strategies for the Sahel, 1975*; later on referred to as *Working Papers: Bellagio Conference*.

42. *Ibid.*, 19.

43. *Ibid.*, 10.

44. *Ibid.*, 17.

45. The alternative view has been expressed by B. W. Hodder, who advocated large-scale sedentarization of the nomads affected by the recent drought; see: 'A note on not perpetuating the status quo', *African Affairs*, vol. 73, 1974, 159–61.

46. *Working Papers: Bellagio Conference*, 25.

47. *Ibid.*, 10, 22, 25.

48. *Ibid.*, 5, 49.

49. *Ibid.*, Appendix C, 40.

50. *Ibid.*, 42.

51. *Ibid.*, 44.

52. S. Baier, *loc. cit.*, 10.

53. ECOWAS includes fifteen West African States; the only Sahel country not participating in the agreement is Chad.

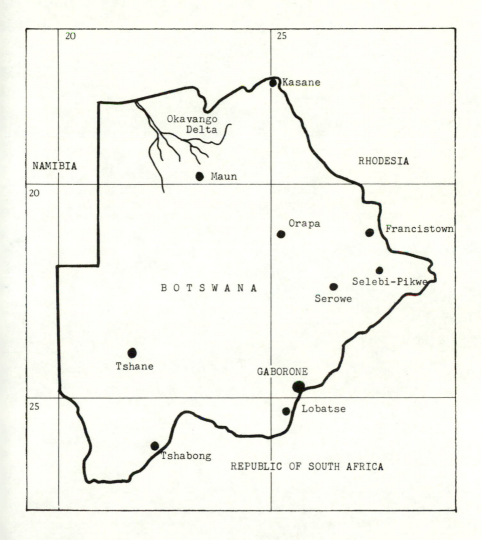

Chapter Six

TRANSHUMANCE: THE CASE OF BOTSWANA

The Development of Trade in Livestock

The territories situated in Southern Africa between latitudes 18° and 27° S., and between longitudes 21° and 28° E., inhabited mostly by the Tswana people, were proclaimed a British Protectorate in 1885. Ten years later its southern part, including the capital town of Mafeking, was transferred to Cape Colony. In 1966 the Protectorate achieved independence and its name was changed from Bechuanaland to Botswana.

The country occupies an area of 581,730 square kilometres, and in 1971 it had a population of 630,000. Climatically, the territory of Botswana is located mostly in the semi-arid and arid zones, ranging from the areas bounded by the isohyets of 250 mm to 650 mm. The south-western part of the country bounded roughly by the 400 mm isohyet in the east, is an extension of the Kalahari sands. It suffers from the absence of surface water, as a result it is very sparsely inhabited. The northern and south-eastern parts of the country enjoy the highest annual precipitation. Extending over an area of 8,000 square kilometres in the north are the Okavango swamps. Here a large shallow depression, occupied by the deltas of the Okavango and Chobe Rivers is covered with aquatic grassland and subject to seasonal floods. The Okavango swamps and some areas of the territory adjacent to it are not suitable for cattle grazing because of the prevalence of the tsetse fly. The remaining parts of Botswana are covered by tree and shrub savannah and the natural conditions there favour livestock raising, though when overgrazing takes place this land turns into a thornbush savannah.[1] The greatest concentration of both the rural and urban population is found in the more humid south-eastern regions.

Botswana is a case study of a country whose population depends largely on livestock raising and to a limited extent on cultivation. But unlike in the countries previously studied, where the majority of the pastoralists lead a nomadic life, in Botswana rural people are village dwellers and their pastoral activities assume the form of transhumance. The importance of pastoralism is indicated by the fact that, at the beginning of the present decade, over 90 per cent of the inhabitants were in the agricultural sector, but less than one-tenth of them were cultivators.

Generally, cattle and small-stock are kept at grazing-posts in the open veld. Smaller settlements keep their cattle-posts near home; elsewhere cattle may be kept up to one hundred miles away from home. Most of the grazing land represents common property and the pastoralists may establish their cattle-posts wherever they wish outside the arable zones. The watering points are used in common, but a person sinking a well or building a dam acquires exclusive rights over the water provided by it.

As a rule the animals are looked after by the sons of the owner while wealthy men employ herdsmen. The location of the posts changes periodically. In the dry season (May–October) the herds are kept closer to the watering points, but when the rains come (November–April) they are moved away and the livestock is grazed freely over the pastures. After the harvest (July–August in the north and May–June in the south) herds are allowed to graze on the stubble in the fields.[2]

In the pre-colonial times the BaTswana people were largely self-sufficient, although some measure of barter took place. Livestock represented the only form in which it was practicable to accumulate wealth. Cattle, and sometimes sheep, were given as bridewealth. The more livestock a man had the more wives he could marry and their labour provided him with more corn.[3]

The custom of lending out his cattle enabled a wealthy man to simplify herding, and reduced the risk of losing his herds through contagious disease or raids. At the same time this practice permitted him to acquire supporters who rendered certain services to him. The holder of 'loan-cattle' would use the milk of the cows and occasionally receive the gift of a heifer.[4] During the colonial period the sale of livestock for local consumption and for export became the principal source of cash income. Africans rarely slaughtered their cattle for food. On the other hand, the consumption of meat by the small European population was insignificant. Consequently the main outlet for livestock trade was found in exporting it to the neighbouring territories.[5] In the 1920s Bechuana cattle were sold to the Union of South Africa, the Rhodesias, Angola, the Belgian Congo, and were even exported overseas to meet the needs of the Italian army.

Exports of livestock from Bechuanaland encountered many obstacles. It was a continuous uphill struggle against animal diseases, drought, and restrictions placed by foreign countries on imports.

The European farmers began to settle in the Protectorate after the epidemic of rinderpest of 1895—96, which is believed to have killed nearly 90 per cent of the cattle population. In 1905 lungsickness made its appearance, and an outbreak of east-coast fever in the adjacent territories led to the imposition of restrictions on the import of livestock to the Cape Colony – Bechuanaland's best market. After 1909, the ban was extended to the whole of the Union of South Africa, and it lasted until 1923. A year later, in an attempt to protect the local farming interests, the import of cattle for sale in the open market was prohibited. Moreover, the remaining market for slaughter cattle was limited by the imposition of weight restrictions. The live weight standards were gradually raised to five hundred kilograms for oxen, and 380 kilograms for cows.[6] The weight standards favoured exports of cattle raised by European farmers. During the 1920s and in the early 1930s the average share of European-owned cattle in the total numbers exported was nearly 7 per cent.[7]

During the 1930s livestock exports suffered a severe setback as a result of dwindling markets and depressed prices.[8]

Faced with these obstacles, both the European and the African farmers who were settled within a reasonable distance of the railway turned their attention to dairying. Markets for their products were found in the Union and in the Rhodesias. The appointment of a dairy expert and inspector in 1926 resulted in considerable progress in the industry. During the period between 1927 and 1931, the output of African-produced butter-fat, which was the most important dairy product, increased from 19,700 kilograms to 93,400 kilograms, whereas that of the Europeans rose from 145,700 kilograms to 264,300 kilograms.[9] In 1931, the value of export of dairy products amounted to 29 per cent of the value of all exports of animal origin. After the Second World War, the relative importance of livestock products decreased.

1927–28 was the first year which registered satisfactory trade statistics. During that period live animals and livestock products exported were valued at £257,000, of which the cattle alone accounted for £138,000. These commodities constituted 89 per cent of the total value of exports. With the exception of the years during which raging animal epidemics prevented the export of cattle, this high percentage was maintained till recent times.

The post-war years brought a rapid increase in the value of livestock exports. Between 1946 and 1955 alone exports rose from £604,300 to £1,948,000. In 1955, there was a drastic change in the composition of exports as a result of the opening of a modern abattoir at Lobatse. A year earlier the Protectorate exported live cattle to the value of £1,443,000 and frozen meat to the value of £118,500. Starting with 1955, export of frozen meat rose to £1,378,500 and the value of live cattle exported fell to £100,000. In 1970, livestock and livestock products still accounted for 88 per cent of the total value of exports. Two years later, when the value of exported minerals rose to 44 per cent, livestock and its products dropped to 49 per cent. This relative decline took place in spite of the fact that there was a continuous increase in the absolute value of exports of animal origin.[10]

Changes in the size of the livestock population form a background for the growth of the potential and the actual off-take. Until 1944 the livestock population figures were scanty and of a highly tentative nature. The size of the cattle herd in Bechuanaland prior to 1895 is not known, but it was estimated that only 10 per cent of it survived the scourge of rinderpest of 1895–96. After the disaster the cattle population recovered steadily, reaching the figure of 139,000 by 1904 and 324,000 heads by 1911. 1914 was the year of the worst drought in the history of Bechuanaland. As a result as much as one third of the livestock had perished in some districts. In 1921, a census disclosed 426,000 heads of cattle and ten years later an estimated figure of 777,000 was reached, of which 693,000 heads or 89 per

Diagram 6.1 Botswana: Livestock Numbers, 1960–1972/73

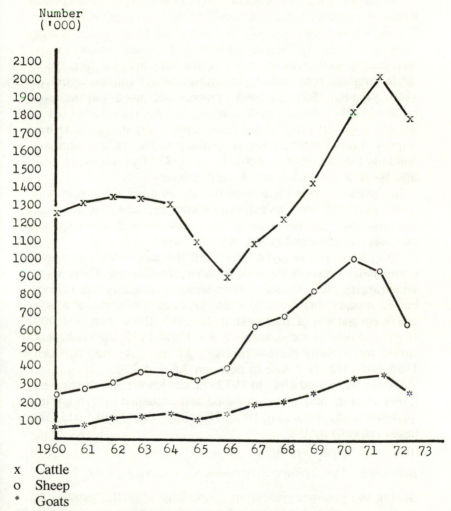

x Cattle
o Sheep
* Goats

Source: Republic of Botswana, Statistical Abstract 1974.

cent was African-owned, and the remaining 84,000 belonged to European farmers.[11] At that time there were 3.55 animals per head of the African and as many as 49.53 per head of the European population.

Towards the end of the Second World War, systematic annual livestock censuses were initiated. The first data published were for 1944 and showed a cattle population of 897,000 and a goat population of 568,000 heads. As from 1947, sheep numbers were included as well. From the end of the war into the late 1950s cattle numbers rose steadily, reaching the 1.3 million figure in 1958. Between 1959 and 1965 numbers fluctuated, but the level remained above the one million mark. In 1966 the number fell to an overall low of 916,000 due to an acute drought. As conditions improved rapid recovery set in resulting in the cattle population reaching the two million mark in 1971–72. The following year this figure was reduced to 1.8 million heads.

In the early 1930s the annual off-take of cattle for export was about three per cent; twenty years later the rate had doubled, reaching over ten per cent in the 1960s, which indicated an increasing commercialization of the livestock sector.

The post-war data show that until the early 1970s the goat numbers far exceeded those of the sheep population. There were wide-ranging fluctuations in both series throughout the period, but it appears that for a decade, or even more, there was a consistent pattern of relationship. In 1947, there were 188,000 sheep and over twice as many goats. Until 1955, the coefficient varied within fairly narrow limits of 2.0 and 2.4; then between 1956 and 1970–71 it rose to between 2.6 and 3.3.

During the period 1947 to 1972–73, the lowest and the highest levels of sheep and goat population were attained in 1960, with 88,000 and 251,000 and in 1970–71, with 370,000 and 1,015,000 heads respectively.[12]

Botswana's Development Programmes: A Reassessment

During the post-war years, and especially after the gaining of independence, development planning played an increasingly important role in Botswana's livestock economy. The present section will assess the more important aspects of the relevant planning strategies.

Planning techniques adopted in the Protectorate since 1946 had to be based on a pragmatic approach, the main reason being an absence of adequate statistical services. At the time of the launching of the 1963–68 Programme the situation had not changed materially.[13]

In view of the rapid constitutional advance and the achievement of independence in 1966, the five-year development programme was replaced by a Transitional Plan covering a three-year period 1966–1969. The new programme was intended to provide for a transition from a rudimentary public expenditure approach to full resource planning. Further work on national planning was delayed by developments in the mining sector, which created a very fluid situation and thwarted work on the long-term projections. Eighteen months after its publication the Transitional Plan was replaced by a new programme extending over the years 1968–73. In 1970 another plan covering the period 1970–75 was introduced, to be followed, three years later, by the 1973–78 National Development Plan.[14] It is, therefore, not possible to think of Botswana's planning process in terms of complete five year plans, as in actual fact the practice of a rolling plan has been followed. In the light of changed circumstances, acquired experience and additional information, continuous revisions are being made and every three years a new document is prepared which sets out the revised policies and programmes.

Planning in Botswana has to be viewed in the light of that country's level of development and the peculiarities of the structure of its economy. In the framework of the international strategy for development, during the Second United Nations Development Decade, Botswana was placed in the group of least developed countries. At that time Botswana's per capita income was below the cut-off point of US$100, and a number of other indicators, such as the share of manufacturing in GDP, and the literacy rate, pointed to a low level of development. In the light of some additional criteria Botswana came out worse than many other less developed countries of Africa. For instance, in 1970 the average electricity consumption per head was 19 Kwh as against an average of 107 Kwh in the other less developed African economies outside the least developed group. Other indices pointed to similar disparities. The density of roads per 1000 square kilometres was 14 kilometres as compared to an average of

39 kilometres. The structure of production tells a similar story. In 1971, Botswana's share of agriculture in her GDP was 47 per cent as against an average of 30 per cent in the other group of countries. Moreover, Botswana's agriculture employed 91 per cent of the total labour force as against an average of 72 per cent in the less developed African countries.

There are also problems resulting from low population density, which approximates one person per square kilometre and is the lowest in sub-Saharan Africa. Hence the per capita cost of administration and other essential services is high compared to that of more compact and densely populated territories. The deficiency of both human and material resources is largely explicable by the aridity of its climate and is aggravated by its dependence on neighbouring countries for access to the sea.

By contrast, in 1971 Botswana's exports of goods and services represented 27 per cent of her GDP, and amounted to US$40 per capita, as against 25 per cent and US$37 average for the developing African countries outside the least developed group.[15] There is a hope that Botswana may be in a position to transform her traditional economy through further expansion of her exports.

The most recent economic developments in Botswana are the result of the discovery of copper-nickel deposits in 1964, which led to further prospecting and new significant discoveries at Pikwe. Also, diamond deposits were discovered in the Orapa area in 1967. In the early 1970s mineral production began in these areas and is now rapidly expanding.

Since 1972–73 revenue from the new mines and higher customs receipts have helped to eliminate substantial deficits in the Government's recurrent budget, which had persisted in earlier years. Mining developments have contributed to an increase in GDP (at market prices) from R47.9 million in 1968–69 to R100.4 million in 1971–72.[16] In addition to diamonds and copper-nickel, which are the most important mineral resources, exploitable deposits of manganese, talc, coal, brine and gypsum have also been discovered.

The mineral discoveries of the 1960s radically changed the economic prospects of Botswana. At the same time, new problems were created, the solution of which called for major revisions in the strategy of development planning in that country.

A study of development planning in Botswana shows quite clearly that each successive plan was a marked improvement on its predecessor, as it provided more detailed statements of national policies as well as more specific targets and objectives for each sector. The quality of planning distinguishes Botswana favourably from many other countries at a similar level of development. It is particularly true of the present statistical basis and the use of projections. For instance, an estimate of the annual growth rate of the GDP was attempted in the Development Plan 1968–73. The projected rate of between 6 and 10 per cent in actual fact has reached 15 per cent in real terms. Not only did it exceed the most optimistic expectations, but the pace of progress put Botswana ahead of other African economies.[17] This considerable underestimation stemmed from the fact that the impact of mining development had not been adequately foreseen. The present Programme is based on an adjusted rate of growth of 14 per cent. Assuming that the population increases at 3 per cent per annum, the annual rate of growth of real per capita income is 11 per cent.[18]

In the past, actual development expenditure tended to fall well below the planned levels. The Transitional Plan was only 57 per cent fulfilled. The development expenditure over the years 1968–1973 amounted to R53.0 million (in 1970 prices) as compared with the target of R71.4 million indicated in the Second National Development Plan (1968–73). This represented a 74 per cent expenditure achievement in that period.[19]

Botswana's planning authorities admit that these disparities between their financial projections and the actual achievement were the result of a deliberate policy on their part. Over-ambitious goals were established deliberately in order to realize the minimal foreign aid requirement. But even with the external resources available for development, the lack of absorptive capacity appeared to be a major obstacle. The delays were mainly due to the time needed for project preparation and institutional and manpower constraints. The rate of implementation improved after 1971 as a result of bilateral agreements for the provision of capital and technical assistance.

The development expenditure planned by the current Programme amounts to R215.3 million, as compared with the previous Programme's expenditure of R95.2 million. This dramatic increase can largely be explained in terms of the government revenue projections. The revenue is expected to grow at 10 per cent per annum, rising from R39 million in 1973–74 to R57 million in 1977–78. The estimated recurrent budget surpluses, which will reach R45 million in the final year, will be used to finance a major part of the development programme. The optimism of these projections has its source in the anticipated growth of revenue from customs, excise and sales duties under the 1969 Customs Union Agreement, as well as from the mining projects, and from the expansion which will take place in the economy at large.[20]

The sectoral distribution of capital expenditure reflects the importance of mineral development. Whereas the absolute amounts of expenditure were increasing rapidly, though unevenly, the share of the various sectors in total public investment followed a different pattern. There is a marked contrast between the sectoral distribution of capital expenditure in the Transitional Plan and the latest Development Programme, particularly in terms of the planned investment in the physical infrastructure which rose from a little over one-third to nearly two-thirds of total expenditure. Shashe Project, closely linked with the Selebi-Pikwe mineral complex, was largely responsible for this change. The share of the investment in social infrastructure and agriculture was nearly halved, during the period under consideration, to about 13 and 8 per cent respectively, while public capital expenditure on the development of commerce and industry (other than mining) slightly reduced its share of the total expenditure.

The private sector's investment during the period 1973–78 has been projected at R80 million, 37.5 per cent of which will be in mining, 18.7 per cent in agriculture, 15.0 per cent in manufacturing, 3.8 per cent in tourism and 25.0 per cent in the remaining parts of the economy.[21]

The general impression of Botswana's development planning in the 1970s is that the decisions concerning the distribution of public capital expenditure on development projects have been primarily influenced by short- or medium-term considerations. It is a common feature of the planning process in many African countries, and Botswana is not an exception, that the approach lacks perspective. Their programmes represent a largely uncoordinated mixture of short-, medium- and long-term projects. Medium-term plans tend to be over-crowded with projects that could become meaningful only if incorporated in a perspective plan embracing several such medium-term plans. It is therefore difficult to see how, in the absence of a long term-plan, Botswana's population policy, education policy, natural resources management, and above all long-term structural changes can be dealt with adequately. This lack of perspective is bound to lead to serious problems in the future, as too little attention is paid to the consistency and continuity of long-term economic policies.[22] In fairness to Botswana's planners it has to be said that the rapid economic change resulting from the recent mineral discoveries made the task of long-term forecasting and planning particularly difficult.

A more basic weakness is the lack of sufficient statistical information. Planners generally tend to base their analysis on macro-economic aggregates derived from national accounts data. Analysis in terms of regions or socio-economic groups is often too superficial and fragmentary. There is a crying need for extensive socio-economic research to be undertaken, which would not only reveal what is going on in the various parts of the economy and what are the responses to development efforts, but which would also assist in the understanding of how the system works.

Botswana's development strategy has been largely determined by an acute shortage of capital and skilled manpower, on the one hand, and the presence of significant natural resources, on the other. Consequently the Government adopted a two-pronged approach: (1) to secure rapid and large returns from investment in mining and other viable industries, mainly aimed at export markets, and (2) to reinvest the revenue from these sources in (a) education and training, (b) agriculture and labour-intensive manufacturing industries, and (c) the improvement of services in the rural areas.[23]

One can hardly argue with these objectives except that what is said in the Programme, in terms of projects and their timing, does not seem to go far enough. It is particularly true when an attempt is made to discover explicit indications as to how some of the key economic objectives are to be realized. These objectives are: the raising of the standard of living of the inhabitants of Botswana, the maximization of the number of new jobs and the promotion of equitable distribution of income.[24]

Mineral development, which is being promoted in order to achieve the fastest possible rate of economic growth, is based on the exploitation of non-renewable resources. To preserve and to increase the wealth of the country the income accruing from this source should be turned into a judiciously selected mix of productive assets. The choice and the timing of such an investment is decisive in averting the dangers inherent in the rapidly changing economic structure. What are these dangers? In the 1960s Botswana's economy was characterized by a low degree of dualism. The change which is now taking place and is stimulated by the present pattern of investment, both in the public and private sectors, will strengthen dualism and intensify income differentials. Statistical data indicate that in 1971–72 the poorest 70 per cent of Botswana's population received 25 per cent of GDP.[25] As the results of recent research show, economic dynamism at low levels of development works to the relative disadvantage of lower income groups. At the same time, it benefits the small and usually expatriate elites.[26] Unless efficient and timely measures are taken, the poorest 70 per cent of Botswana's population will become even poorer. The process of pauperization will be enhanced by the high rate of population growth which has attained 3 per cent per annum in the recent years.[27]

Projections, based on varying assumptions, indicate that the 1971 population of 630,000 will in the year 2001 reach a level somewhere between a lower limit of 1,000,000 (based on the assumptions of declining fertility and continued emigration) and an upper limit of 1,646,000 (based on the assumptions of constant fertility and no emigration).[28] Emigration, which was a significant factor in the past, cannot be counted upon in the more distant future. The importance of the employment problem in the years to come cannot be underestimated. It is envisaged that during the period 1973–78 an average of 5,300 new jobs will be created annually, which gives a total employment figure of 80,000 by 1978. It is claimed by the planners that the years beyond 1978 are too distant to make an accurate estimate of employment. However, it has been indicated that between 1978 and 1988 some slowing down in the rate of growth of GDP will be reflected in the rate of growth of formal sector employment. A tentative target for employment in 1988 would be 140,000, which translates into an average of 6,000 new jobs per year between 1978 and 1988. This implies a drop in the employment growth rate from 8.8 per cent per annum during 1973–78 to between 5.0 and 6.0 per cent over the period 1978–88. During the period of the current Programme about 80 per cent of the annual increase in Botswana's resident active labour force is being absorbed in the formal sector's employment. In the subsequent period the rates of unemployment and underemployment will be increasing more rapidly.[29]

The precariousness of Botswana's employment situation is reflected in the proportion of her labour force seeking work in South Africa. This migrant group of workers, estimated at nearly 50,000, cannot count on continued employment opportunities abroad. Moreover, this form of 'labour export' is not in keeping with Botswana's concept of economic independence.

Criticism of planning strategy cannot be constructive unless concrete proposals on the synchronization of the short- and long-term objectives are formulated. An analysis of Botswana's natural resources, apart from mineral wealth, indicates a considerable development potential. Botswana has a large area of semi-arid lands suited for grazing. These lands are either unutilized because of poor accessibility, or they are underutilized because of the lack of scientifically controlled approach to their exploitation. A rational approach to range management is hampered by the existing land tenure system which relies on the communal use of unfenced grazing land.

In the late 1960s the national herd numbered about one and a half million head of cattle, with an off-take averaging 10 per cent per annum. It has been suggested that, assuming constant prices, it should be possible to increase the herd size by fifty per cent and raise the off-take by a similar percentage within two decades, thus doubling the income from cattle.[30] With less conservative assumptions about improvements in productivity and the world market prices for beef the results could be very different.

The contribution of small-stock to the nation's diet is also important and could be greatly increased. But the production of meat is only one aspect of livestock raising. It has been claimed that 600,000 trek oxen would be required in order to fully utilize Botswana's available arable land. Furthermore, the national herd could increase its contribution to the nation's nutrition in the form of dairy products.[31] Animal husbandry could also provide valuable raw materials for the various branches of the manufacturing industry.

It is beyond the scope of this study to discuss the ways and means of increasing the productivity of animal husbandry and augmenting the size of the national herd. The main lines of approach may be mentioned merely as a matter of interest. The above aims could be realized by:

(a) increasing off-take and lowering the age of slaughtered animals;

(b) raising the average weight of animals by the provision of adequate transport and the more widespread use of finishing ranches where cattle are fattened for a fee;

(c) improving calving percentage (at present 45 per cent);

(d) improving the distribution of boreholes and controlling their utilization;

(e) making good mineral deficiencies particularly with regard to phosphorus, sodium and chlorine;

(f) developing methods of range management conducive to sustained production.

Improvement in marketing arrangements would provide incentives to producers to raise the quality of livestock and to make them more willing to sell their animals. As in the past, the trading of cattle is of considerable importance as a source of cash income to a large proportion of the people of Botswana. It has been estimated that in the early 1970s the inhabitants of the Kalahari earned annually approximately R6 million from this source, which provided them with a per capita figure close to R50.[32] With further improvements that income could be considerably increased.

Livestock also provides an important part of food supply. According to rough estimates people in the Kalahari consume annually 36.5 kilograms of meat per head, from domestic animals.[33] The consumption of milk is at least 200 litres per head and large quantities of hides and skins are used.[34] It follows that the development of the existing potential could lead to significant increase in both money and subsistence income.

The Botswana Meat Commission acts as a marketing board and has a monopoly of the processing of meat for export. Prices paid by the Commission to the producers are rising rapidly, reflecting the improvement in the quality and the trend in the world beef price of recent years. Producers are assured of a market for their animals at prices announced at the beginning of each year. The question is: can they take full advantage of the existing marketing arrangements? Most of the producers have to travel long distances in order to reach the export abattoir at Lobatse. Trekking is extremely hazardous because of limited and irregular water supplies and grazing. Trucking, whenever available, appears to be expensive, so many farmers sell livestock locally to intermediaries at low prices.[35] The latter frequently enjoy a monopsonistic position and collaborate with big buyers.

The problem of transportation could be solved by providing adequate road transport and the construction of a second abattoir, the location of which would depend on future export markets. At present, the construction of a second abattoir would reduce the advantages resulting from the economies of scale realized at Lobatse. With a smaller turnover overheads per animal slaughtered would rise to the detriment of producer prices.[36] The final outcome would depend on whether the gains from reduced costs of transport would exceed the loss caused by higher costs of slaughterhouse operations. Eventually with the expansion in the numbers of animals offered for export both abattoirs could achieve an optimal operational size.

Whilst the development of livestock production in Botswana could provide the rural population with additional incomes and better diet it is unlikely that it would have strong job-creating effects. The livestock industry is not labour-intensive and the system of cattle-posts enables a relatively small number of herdsmen to take care of a large number of animals on a communal basis. Increased meat exports would lead to some job creation in the transportation industry and in the abattoirs. Some forward linkage effects would be present in directions suggested by a further utilization of raw materials of animal origin other than meat, but these are not likely to be of much significance from the point of view of employment.

It is important to ensure that the benefits of increased productivity become widespread. This can be achieved if the base of livestock ownership is sufficiently broadened. The rural sector's per capita income of R50 is far below the national average of R142 (based on 1971–72 GDP at factor cost). Being an average it masks the degree of maldistribution of ownership of cattle. The data for 1971–72 indicate that 32 per cent of traditional farmers had no cattle at all; another 26 per cent had 10 or less heads each, whilst 17 per cent owned between 11 and 20 heads. Only 25 per cent of farmers owned 21 animals or more. As many as 16 per cent of farmers did not produce any grain and of that number 3.7 per cent did not own cattle either.[37]

The distribution of wealth in the form of cattle is not the same thing as the distribution of income. There are several traditional ways in which income of the wealthy livestock owners may be redistributed. This may happen through paid employment of poorer farmers, through extended family ties, or through the *mafisa* system.[38] On the other hand, there are circumstances which have an adverse effect on the distribution of cattle ownership. It is believed that the years of drought tend to intensify the maldistribution of cattle ownership as the biggest losses occur in the East where smaller herds prevail. Apart from drought, overstocking is also a problem. The combined effect of these two factors, after each successive drought, produces ever greater fluctuations in the size of the cattle population and a further polarization in the distribution of cattle ownership.[39]

The problem is magnified by the fact that under the present system of borehole utilization owners of the larger cattle herds are able to acquire effective rights to use land which becomes inaccessible to the smaller cattle owners.

Another feature of the present system is the prevalence of communal grazing areas. From this point of view Botswana shares the same problems as a number of other African countries discussed in this study. Approximately 90 per cent of the national herd resides in the lands where improved range management cannot be introduced. For instance, traditional prohibition against fencing on tribal land is still practised. Consequently, efficient livestock production practices are limited largely to the freehold farming areas.

The rapid growth of livestock population in recent years has led to more exhaustive exploitation of the traditional grazing lands, which has caused their progressive degradation. It has been realized that these problems will become more acute unless the Government intervenes by enforcing institutional changes, necessary for the improvement of the standards of range management and efficient control over livestock numbers.

The next section deals with governmental initiatives intended to effect the reform of the existing system.

National Policy on Tribal Grazing Land

The enactment of the Tribal Land Act in 1968 was the first step taken in the introduction of a land tenure system compatible with the changed conditions in agriculture. This Act established Tribal Land Boards and endowed them with the right to allocate land, which had been exercised till then by the local chiefs. This new law came into force in 1970. According to it, land ownership remains with the tribe but the right to use the land is registered in the names of individuals.[40] A further step undertaken by the Government was the formulation of an outline of a policy on tribal grazing land, which was set forth in Government Paper No. 2 of 1973, entitled 'National Policy for Rural Development'. The basic aims were

> to stop overgrazing and degradation of the veld; to promote greater equality of incomes in the rural areas; and to allow growth and commercialization of the livestock industry on a sustained basis.

The authorities were quite explicit in their statements as to what should be done. They were less clear as to how their intentions should be carried out. There was a fear that errors of judgement made in the early stages of implementation would be hard to rectify in the later stages. It was not until 1975 that the Government outlined the measures deemed necessary to realize these aims, which were declared as 'national policy on tribal grazing land'.[41] The new document emphasizes the need for a change of the present system. In recent years the cattle population has increased rapidly in response to the favourable beef prices, and unprecedented numbers of animals were marketed. Unfortunately, this otherwise positive development produced two undesirable side effects. Firstly, under the system of uncontrolled grazing, the increase in livestock led to serious overgrazing around villages, surface water sources and boreholes. The most severely affected were the small cattle owners, whose herds graze around village areas. Secondly, the wealthier cattle owners, who could afford to drill boreholes, secured virtual control over the newly opened grazing land, whereas cattle owners possessing only a few heads of cattle stayed in the overcrowded village areas with little hope of improvement. Under these conditions the reallocation of grazing land and the introduction of rational methods of range management became imperative. To achieve these aims groups and individuals must be granted exclusive rights to land by dividing the grazing areas into three distinct zones, which will differ in terms of tenure and the type of development. They will include: (1) commercial farming areas; (2) communal grazing areas; and (3) reserved areas.

The allocation of grazing land among these three categories will be carried out by the Land Boards, which will be also entrusted with the execution of the policy. Their decisions will have to take into consideration local differences. The Boards will be guided by the Government in their task.

The document referred to above provides guidelines and rules for the three zones.[42] Land in the commercial farming areas will cease to be used communally, and exclusive rights, based on leases subject to the payment of rent, will be vested in groups or individuals. It is expected that some areas where individual or group control over blocks of land has already been established, such as sandveld cattle-posts, will be classified as commercial, unless a good reason is given for including them in the communal zones.

Decisions as to how much land should be set aside for commercial farming areas will be taken after an investigation has been made into the requirements for communal, reserved, and other land. Such requirements will include the estimated demands for different categories of land over the next fifty years. It is also proposed that no commercial lease should include a borehole, unless satisfactory watering arrangements are provided for the owners of livestock currently using it.

A clear indication is given as to who should be accorded priority when leases are granted. First of all, allocations of grazing land will be made to individuals and groups who own a specified minimum number of animals. Furthermore, preference will be given to groups of smaller owners intending to run commercial ranches, rather than to large individual cattle owners. Pastoralists from overstocked communal lands will be encouraged to transfer their herds to commercial areas. Priority will be assigned to those who are not yet holding any commercial leases. When granting new leases, each Land Board will take into account the total land holding of an applicant in all parts of Botswana. As a result of the assessment of the existing land holdings, owners of a large number of boreholes may be asked to surrender some of them.

Provisions will be made to discourage speculation in leases and other forms of misuse of the grazing land.[43] Leases will be granted for a period of fifty years and restrictions will be imposed on their transfer, except when the interests of those who have provided loan finance have to be safeguarded. Subletting and sub-division of holdings will require the approval of the Land Board, but no limitations will be placed on the inheritance of a lease.[44]

The second category of zoning consists of the communal grazing areas, where the communal grazing system will be permitted to continue and no payments of rent will be required. These areas will lie near the villages.[45] The maximum number of livestock that may be kept by a person, family, or group on a given communal land area will be determined by the appropriate Land Board, and animals kept under the *mafisa* system will be counted as belonging to the holder.

The drilling of new, privately owned, boreholes will not be permitted in communal areas, and the boreholes where owners are watering more stock than permitted by the Land Board will be phased out.

Overcrowding will be remedied (a) by the extension of the area of communal grazing land, and (b) by the removal to the commercial farming areas of owners whose herds exceed the maximum size as stipulated by the Board. Small owners who are organized into livestock management groups will be permitted to fence the land allocated to them in the communal grazing areas.[46]

The third category of zoning consists of the reserved areas, which are to be set aside for future use by the growing population as well as such alternative uses as wildlife, mining and cultivation.[47]

At the time of writing no legislation has yet been passed along the lines suggested in the Government Paper.[48]

There is little doubt that Botswana's new national policy on tribal grazing land is a major step forward in the right direction. Its success will depend on the swift enforcement of the proposed legislation and the faithful interpretation of the spirit of the law.

The initial reaction of Parliament to the proposed policy statement was favourable. It was felt that the proposal provided for the development of the land and paid adequate attention to the interests of the people who occupy it.[49] Most importantly the right of every tribesman to use as much land as he needs to sustain himself and his family is safeguarded. The idea that the traditional attitude to land use should be subject to revision is fully supported. But the individualistic concept of personal property need not be encouraged. If small livestock owners organize themselves into groups they can enjoy the benefits of the large-scale farmer, improved stock, fencing, loans for development, better marketing facilities, etc.[50] In Botswana pastoral activities are largely organized on a communal basis and this paves the way for a widespread application of cooperative system which has already enjoyed some measure of success in the field of marketing. The State Lands represent over 48 per cent of the total area of the country and can provide land for this type of communal organization.[51]

There are some who fear that the division of the land into grazing zones would create conditions under which the small owners are forced to move out to be replaced by the rich landlords.[52] It will depend on the honesty of the Land Boards in their implementation of the national policy, whether these fears are justified. The Government is aware of the problem but it believes that through careful planning and through consultation with the people such dangers can be avoided. The Land Boards can play a crucial role in closing the gap between rich and poor, and in securing adequate incomes not only for the present, but also for future generations of cattle-raisers. One of their important tasks will be to fix the rents at a level which reflects the value of the natural resources used by the herders.

The sequence of implementation as indicated in the Government Paper No. 2 of 1975 gives priority to the identification of areas which are suitable for commercial development, to allow a speedy removal of some of the larger herds from the communal village grazing lands and to enable those who acquire commercial allocations to begin developing their ranches.

Some of the problems arising out of the implementation of the programme will be subject to a further study by the Government. These are: the availability of public transport, water equipment and fencing materials, the road network, borehole maintenance, social infrastructure and the implications for the settlement patterns of the future of the freehold and state land policy.[53]

Botswana's policy with regard to the tribal grazing land has not yet been subject to a test under the existing conditions. It is designed along lines which appear to be both sound and practicable and it hopes to find a solution to the special problems which face the pastoral sector of the economy.

The applicability of similar policies in other economies is circumscribed by differences in the forms of pastoralism practiced. Widespread transhumance combined with the Government's control over wide, and largely unutilized, stretches of potential range create conditions for legal and economic solutions based on Botswana's model.

NOTES

1. I. Schapera, *The Tswana*. London: International African Institute, 1962; 23–4.
2. *Financial and Economic Position of the Bechuanaland Protectorate*. Report of the Commission Appointed by the Secretary of State for Dominion Affairs, 1933, Cmd. 4368; 6.
3. I. Schapera, *Married Life in an African Tribe*. London: Faber and Faber Ltd., 1940; 118.
4. *Ibid.*, 120.
5. The off-take of animals for local consumption in the Protectorate could not be estimated. Even such imperfect indicators as the number of hides and skins sold is not available, as only total money values for these items were recorded.
6. *Financial and Economic Position of the Bechuanaland Protectorate*; 14–16.
7. *Ibid.*, Appendix 6; 161.
8. *Ibid.*, 15–16.
9. *Ibid.*, 16, Appendices 5 and 6.
10. International Monetary Fund, *Surveys of African Economies*, vol. 5, Washington, D.C.: IMF, 1973; 92; Republic of Botswana, *National Development Plan 1973–78*, Part 1; 24.
11. *Financial and Economic Position of the Bechuanaland Protectorate*; 25–6.
12. Bechuanaland: *Annual Colonial Report 1955*; Republic of Botswana, *Statistical Abstract 1974*.
13. Bechuanaland: *Report for the year 1964*. London: HMSO, 1965; 10.
14. Another Development Plan has been announced but it was not yet available at the time of writing.

15. United Nations, *Survey of Economic Conditions in Africa 1972*, Part 1, New York 1973; 280.
16. Barclays Country Reports: *Botswana*, 4th November 1974.
17. The Transitional Plan did not contain any projections of GDP since, at that time, national accounts data was not yet available. GDP (at factor cost) was then roughly estimated at R25 million. Subsequent calculations adjusted that figure upwards to R40 million for 1966–7.
18. Botswana's estimates of GDP per capita and its growth rate are tentative.
19. Republic of Botswana, *National Development Plan 1973–78*, Part 1; 31–2.
20. *Ibid.*, 52.
21. Data based on the *Transitional Plan for Social and Economic Development, 1966*; 52, and the *National Development Plan 1973–78*, Part 1; 40, 333, and Part 2, 127.
22. Criticisms along these lines have been directed against the planning process in other African countries. See *U.N. Survey of Economic Conditions in Africa 1972*; 34–41.
23. Republic of Botswana, *National Development Plan 1973–78*, Part 1; 37.
24. *Ibid.*, xi.
25. Based on statistical data provided in the *National Development Plan 1973–78*, Part 1; 21–2, 41, and *Statistical Abstract 1973*, table 4.
26. I. Adelman and C. T. Morris, *Economic Growth and Social Equity in Developing Countries*. Stanford: Stanford University Press, 1973; 161, 188.
27. *National Development Plan 1973–78*, Part 1; 3.
28. *Ibid.*, table 1.5.
29. *Ibid.*, 87–8.
30. P. M. Landell-Mills, 'The Economy of Botswana – A Review', *Botswana Notes and Records*, Special Edition no. 1, Proceedings of the Conference on Sustained Production from Semi-Arid Areas, October 1971; 25.
31. H. A. Fosbrooke, 'Social Implications of Sustained Livestock Production in the Kalahari', *Botswana Notes and Records*, Special Edition no. 1, October 1971; 181.
32. B. P. Thomson, 'The Current Significance of Livestock Production in the Kalahari', *Botswana Notes and Records*, Special Edition no. 1, October 1971; 124.
33. A corresponding figure estimated by ECA/FAO for selected East African countries is 11.8 kilograms per head.
34. G. L. Cole, 'Livestock Marketing in the Kalahari', *Botswana Notes and Records*, Special Edition no. 1, October 1971; 193.
35. *Ibid.*, 194–5.
36. *Ibid.*, 197.
37. *National Development Plan 1973–78*, Part 1; 22.
38. Under the *mafisa* system the owner of cattle gives some of his animals to someone else to take care of. This service is remunerated in the form of milk, the draught power of the oxen, and possibly a beast when the owner takes his animals back. (H. Metterick, 'The Kalahari in the Context of Rural Development' *Botswana Notes and Records*, Special Edition no. 1, October 1971; 30).

39. B. P. Thomson, *loc. cit.*; 124–5.
40. International Monetary Fund, *Surveys of African Economies*, vol. 5; 37.
41. Republic of Botswana, Government Paper no. 2 of 1975 *'National Policy on Tribal Grazing Land'*.
42. *Ibid.*, 11–14.
43. It is understood that leases will be granted under Section 21 of the Tribal Land Act of 1968, providing safeguards against misuses of the land.
44. Republic of Botswana, *Government Paper No. 2 of 1975*; 15.
45. *Ibid.*, 6.
46. 'Small owners' are defined as those who have fewer animals than the maximum number fixed by the Land Board for individual herders in the communal area.
47. *Ibid.*, 7, 11, 12.
48. Personal communication from the Office of the Director of Botswana Information Services, dated 10th March, 1977.
49. See for example: 'MPs give backing to new land policy', *Botswana Daily News*, July 18, 1975.
50. S. T. Khama, 'Traditional Attitudes to Land and Management of Property with Special Reference to Cattle', *Botswana Notes and Records*, Special Edition no. 1, October 1971; 61.
51. H. A. Fosbrooke, 'Man in the Kalahari: Tribal Areas', *Botswana Notes and Records*, Special Edition no. 1, October 1971; 41.
52. 'MPs give backing to new land policy' *Botswana Daily News*, July 18, 1975.
53. Republic of Botswana, *Government Paper No. 2 of 1975*; 17.

Chapter Seven

SOME SPECULATIONS ON THE PROSPECTS OF THE PASTORAL MODE OF PRODUCTION

And the seven years of plenteousness, that was in the land of Egypt, were ended. And the seven years of dearth began to come, according as Joseph had said: and the dearth was in all lands; but in all the land of Egypt there was bread.

Genesis 41

The Alternatives

Our case studies have shown a considerable degree of uniformity. Human overpopulation already exists in some of the pastoral societies, others are dangerously close to it. Animal overpopulation is the rule in the regions which, with a different system of range management, could become far more productive than they have been before. The age-old pastoral attitudes and institutions survive, resulting in a precarious combination of unrestrained livestock accumulation and the common use of pastures.

An analysis of modern planning methods applied to pastoral sectors points to a persistent use of measures which unintentionally assist the pastoralist in his propensity to hoard animals. The veterinary efforts to reduce livestock mortality coupled with projects aiming at augmenting water supplies tend to further aggravate the situation. The uniformity and repetitiveness of such methods is quite striking. It is disappointing to see how little has been learnt from past experience. With very few exceptions, modern planners have neglected to implement measures which would improve range management, marketing, and above all, bring about the reform of the land tenure system. One of their gravest mistakes was their inability or unwillingness to distinguish more clearly between the short- and long-term approach. It is only in the long run that properly diagnosed socio-economic ills can be treated by dealing with their deeply rooted causes.

A recent example of the dangers of an incomplete and ill-informed approach is the attempt to restore the pre-drought conditions in the Sahel. In spite of the fact that there is a lack of any meaningful new policies and the old ones were inadequate, nomads are being assured that a disaster of the magnitude of the last drought will never be repeated.

The Sahelian drought brought forth suggestions as to the solution of the problem of pastoral nomadism. One of the views was that the *status quo* should not be perpetuated.[1] It recommended that nomads who were affected by the drought should be encouraged to settle permanently in urban and rural areas in the less climatically vulnerable southern stretches of their countries. As the recent drought accelerated trends that have, for some time, been apparent in the region, the nomadic mode of life should be discontinued.[2]

The above approach represents the school of thought whose tenets have already been discussed (see chapter three), and which regards sedentarization as the only rational solution of the human problems of the arid and semi-arid zones. However, new arguments have been put forth in support of these views. It is said that the problem of the Sahel, and of the other rain-deficient pastoral areas of Africa, is primarily a problem of development in its widest sense, and the means at the disposal of the countries which control the region are far from sufficient to solve it. It is naive to suggest that international aid or cooperation between West African states can ever provide the necessary resources.[3]

The difference between the older version of the 'sedentarization solution' and the new one lies in the magnitude of the problem and the conditions under which it is being solved. In the past, sedentarization schemes were implemented in countries where pastoral nomads formed a small proportion of the total population and their absorption into other sectors of the economy was possible. Large-scale sedentarization took place under conditions of a revolutionary 'command economy' which involved a far-reaching reform of the system of ownership and management. This was the case of the Kazakhs in the USSR, and lately of Northern Somalia, where the sedentarization scheme was implemented with the help of foreign aid, but where the number of persons involved was little more than 5 per cent of the total population.

In the Sahel the nomad population that would have to be sedentarized approximates two and one half million. The question is what resources would be needed to perform such a formidable task? Would it not be more realistic to find resources for the economic development of the pastoral sector, rather than to sedentarize it at an enormous cost?

The amount of external aid given to the Sahel at the height of the drought was almost a billion dollars.[4] It is a sad reflection that adequate means are not readily available to prevent disasters in good time. Assistance on an unprecedented scale is only available when it is too late. A more modest development aid, given earlier, would have gone a long way to help solve the development problem of the Sahel.

A list of the drawbacks and dangers of large-scale sedentarization was given in one of the earlier chapters (chapter three). However, there is one more danger which results from the present Sahelian situation. The drought and the consequent hunger led to the economic ruin of the nomads. This opened the way for capitalist transformation of the areas previously occupied by them. Commercial stock farming and the use of hired labour are encouraged. Claude Meillassoux, who represents a radical point of view, claims that both the governments of the affected countries and the powers who give aid do not have a genuine interest at heart to save the local population. All they are concerned with is to slow down the exodus of the nomads to the towns, where difficult social problems may arise, and to diminish their anger caused by destitution. Meillassoux views the famine in Africa as an opening of doors to a cruel but lucrative future for foreign investors.[5]

Fears of this kind are not quite unreasonable, as there is some evidence of the existence of projects concerned with large-scale cattle-ranching, going back to the pre-drought times. Some African governments have been cooperating with North American and European agricultural business interests to create large agro-industrial enterprises endowed with modern equipment and infra-structural facilities including abattoirs, refrigeration plants, and airfields destined to ship out livestock products overseas. These projects involving millions of hectares of rangeland are not limited to the Sahel region alone. They include also a number of East African countries. The large-scale ranchers are not concerned with the possibility of periodic droughts. Human depopulation and modern technology, they feel, will take care of this problem.[6]

Unrestrained capitalistic ranching which would coexist with the traditional forms of pastoral nomadism would be to the detriment of the nomads, by diminishing their lands and contributing to the worsening of their economic situation. Pastoral nomads may find themselves in an untenable position. On the one hand, their existence would be threatened through desertification, unless they adopt conservationist attitudes; on the other hand, they would be subject to unfair competition on the part of foreign investors, who with their enormous commercial ranches would bar their rights to the traditional nomadic free movements.

African countries situated in the rain-deficient zone lack natural resources which would be adequate to effect sedentarization of large numbers of nomads. Even if new resources could be marshalled through irrigation schemes on a substantial scale with the assistance of international aid, such a solution would take too long to avert difficulties which might in the meantime arise. It is more than likely that pastoral nomads would turn into an urban proletariat swelling the ranks of the already destitute slum-dwellers, to become a reservoir of cheap labour. Alternatively they might end by being reduced to the status of permanent and unproductive inhabitants of the displaced persons' camps to be maintained by international agencies at the expense of the foreign taxpayer. Too often it is said that 'people can get used' to conditions which they find initially unacceptable. Thus one can become accustomed to polluted air or to unclean water, one can also accept life in a slum as 'normal'. Especially is this true of the second generation of people who have never known a better way of living. But is it an acceptable approach?

There are further considerations, which are of a decisive nature and which should be taken into account. By altering the factors determining human fertility, settlement is more than likely to raise the rate of growth of the sedentarized population by at least one per cent. In other words, the time within which population doubles would be reduced from about forty-six years for pastoral nomads, to twenty-eight years or less for those nomads who are permanently settled. The implications of this change need no further comments.

In addition, the development of commercial ranching by foreign interests is certain to deprive the local population of the valuable protein content in their diet, forcing it to rely increasingly on carbohydrates. Some African countries, least able to afford it, export livestock and livestock products disregarding the consequences of the lack of proper nutritional policy for the health of their population.[7] In many of the less developed parts of the world the exploitation of the protein resources by the rich countries is parasitic. The use of the anchoveta riches of the Peruvian Current was a typical case in question and the grasslands of tropical Africa have been described as an 'indispensable artificial leg' to the animal industry of Europe.[8]

To conclude, commercial ranching is undesirable if it is in conflict with the interests of the local population. Nevertheless, its potential contribution should not be neglected if it can be developed under the full control of the government.

The analysis of the pastoral sectors of several sub-Saharan economies has shown that there is no simple and prompt remedy for their ills. We have no panacea, and there are no means readily available in the short run to save the nomads. Ill-conceived efforts in this direction lead to the progressive deterioration of the range, which defeats the purpose. On the other hand, saving the range by massive sedentarization means sacrificing the welfare of the nomads. There is no alternative to a gradual approach. Risks must be taken and hopes must be pinned on the chance that droughts will not occur within the next decade or so.

Proposal for Pastoral Reform

Comments dealing with the recent events in the Sahel have a wider application. Differences between the political systems of the countries where pastoralism is predominant play only a limited role. A centrally planned economy, based on a socialist model, may be better suited to protect itself against the excesses of foreign capital than a free market economy, but it is not immune to errors of judgement that may have serious consequences. There are some important similarities between the economies of the countries under consideration. Somalia, Botswana, and the Sahelian countries all have moist zones and considerable stretches of land suitable for irrigation or dry-land grain production. Substantial areas exist which have not yet been opened to human use, but which represent potential pastoral land. Also there are large areas unsuitable for livestock but suitable for wildlife exploitation on a commercial basis. The wide diversity of uses offers possibilities for the solution of the pastoral problem.

Arable land could be used (a) for the production of fodder which in time could serve as an emergency stock for the pastoral sector, and (b) for the fattening of livestock destined for sale. The availability of unused agricultural land and areas where irrigation is possible permits future sedentarization of the nomads and the introduction of mixed farming. On the other hand, unutilized pastoral land can be employed for the organization of commercial ranches. Wherever new grasslands can be brought into pastoral use by the provision of watering facilities or tsetse fly eradication, a new legal framework can be introduced which will permit scientific range management. Areas should be set aside, in the newly opened ranges, which would be government-controlled and used only in case of drought. There are also arid lands where livestock leads a precarious existence, such as the northern fringes of the Sahel, north-eastern Somalia, or parts of the Kalahari Desert in Botswana. Investigations should be made to ascertain whether it would not be more economical to convert these areas into wild ranches rather than to continue their use for domestic livestock. Wild ungulates have feeding habits and possess physiological mechanisms which permit them to survive without drinking water far better than domestic animals. They also have a higher metabolic rate, growing faster at times when food is more readily available. Wild ungulates' meat, therefore, could be produced faster.[9]

Botswana's policy with regard to tribal grazing land could be emulated, with some modifications, by other countries. Through proper legislation unoccupied grazing areas could be set aside for commercial ranching, which would either be run directly by the government, or leased to large livestock owners, or to associations of smaller herders, who would be willing to accept the rules regulating the new ranching units. The latter would then transfer their herds to these areas. The occupiers of commercial ranches would be subject to strict rules of rational range management and safeguards would have to be provided against the excesses of exploitation by foreign investors. Rent payments and taxes would serve as compensation for the benefits derived from the natural resources owned by the society at large. Whereas the opportunity cost of pastoral lands is often nil, the opportunity cost of the resources expended by the society to maintain the ranges in permanent use without deterioration is positive. It is in the interest of the present and the future generations that the pastures remain a fully renewable natural resource.

The concentration of large livestock owners in commercial ranches would solve a number of essential problems. Firstly, efforts to destock other areas would be greatly assisted; secondly, it would enable the public authorities to extend their control over pastoral activities; and lastly it would encourage investment and the application of methods leading to increased productivity, range conservation, and employment of labour. The above policy need not be interpreted as leading to the intensification of disparities in income and wealth. It is true that it would contribute towards the elimination of the traditional redistributive mechanisms. Redistribution could be achieved instead by way of a system of progressive taxation.

Small livestock owners can improve their economic position by forming cooperatives. The idea of owners' associations for the purpose of livestock raising is not new. D. J. Stenning studied the case of owners' associations with regard to the pastoral Fulani of Northern Nigeria and I. Cunnison tried to apply the latter's approach to the Humr people of the Sudan, long before Botswana adopted these associations to solve her own problems of the pastoral sector.[10]

Stenning defined a 'ranch' as a demarcated area expected to support cattle sufficient to sustain a number of inhabitants exercising exclusive rights to specific forms of land use.[11] In his view the aim of the ranching enterprise was to create conditions whereby part of the annual increase in livestock could be regarded as disposable surplus.[12] Both Stenning and Cunnison attempted to identify a social grouping which would be most amenable to the communal operation of a ranch. They stressed the importance of an adequate economic organization, a degree of corporateness, and a leadership capable of managing ranching settlements and disposing of their surplus livestock.[13]

In addition to the first zone occupied by commercial ranches a second major pastoral zone would comprise lands left to the communal use of the pastoral nomads, whose periodic movements depend on the variability of the conditions of the range. There would be two categories of land. One would serve the needs of the semi-nomads who engage in transhumance. Their transhumance orbits are far more restricted than the movements of fully nomadic people. Arrangements similar to those of Botswana's communal grazing areas might be appropriate in their case. A separate type of arrangement would be introduced to serve the needs of the nomads, whose movements are far less defined and far more extensive than those of the semi-nomads.

It is useful, at this stage, to refer to the discussion of the two models of a pastoral community, outlined in the second chapter of this study. At that stage our main preoccupation was with the limits within which the pastoral economy can evolve. Our present interest is directed to the possibility of establishing an optimal situation defined in terms of the desired level of pastoral welfare achievable with the available natural resources.

It was shown then that the closed steady state system, which was the essence of the 'idealized' model, could not be maintained indefinitely. It was necessary, therefore, to replace it with a 'realistic' model, in order to assess the consequences of a positive rate of human population growth which, combined with the traditional tendency to accumulate livestock, leads to the over-stepping of the limits imposed by the availability of rangeland. Apart from human population growth, sources of disequilibrium can be found in the existence of the various links with the rest of the economy, and in the cyclical changes related to the stochastic variations in rainfall.

It was not possible to identify any built-in functional relationships between the variables of the 'realistic' model which would be strong enough to maintain the equilibrium position of a steady state. Even the exogenously determined increases in prices proved insufficient to elicit an adequate rate of off-take. It has also been shown previously that one cannot rely on the effectiveness of efforts aimed at the elimination of the traditional pastoral values favouring livestock accumulation. Instead, regulation appears inevitable. It can be made more acceptable to the nomads by the introduction of schemes demonstrating clearly the advantages accruing to them from the new policy measures.

Given the area of the range, the goal of the maximum sustainable yield stocking density requires the manipulation of a number of variables of which the most crucial ones are the size of the human population and the off-take. They should be controlled in such a way that the animal population is maintained at the desired level. Conditions must also be created for the acceptance by the other sectors of the economy of the redundant pastoralists, and adequate arrangements must be made for the disposal of surplus livestock.

The suggested policy points to a new version of the 'idealized' model. The third model could be justifiably termed 'normative' as it strives to realize the conditions conforming to the norm of a steady state. Within that new framework increases in pastoral welfare can be realized in a number of ways. One of them is an improvement in the relation between selling prices and costs, e.g. through fortuitous upward changes in prices. Another change leading in the desired direction may occur through improvements in productivity. Still another way of achieving that goal is through adjustments in the number of pastoralists within the sector. Once the limit of improvements in efficiency has been reached and no further price increases are envisaged, the achievement of the desired standard of living requires reduction in the number of people.

The rest of the economy will have to implement a sufficient number of projects providing employment which would be attractive enough to overcome the reluctance of prospective settlers. Some of these projects could create income-earning opportunities for mixed farmers, whereby former nomads could combine a transhumant mode of livestock-raising with cultivation.

Direct measures to remove excess human population from the pastoral sector should be discouraged. Instead, indirect control over the size of population may be achieved by restricting the size of the nomadic herds.

In the past, policies applied to the pastoral sector unintentionally facilitated livestock accumulation by the nomads. Increased sales of animals were only a by-product of a higher rate of growth of herds. They were not its most important result. The nomads were expected to abandon their traditional attitudes to livestock but, at the same time, they were offered nothing that could be considered as a substitute which would provide them with a sense of security. They needed a *quid pro quo* in the form of an insurance against the consequences of a major drought.

The principle upon which the policy proposed in this study relies is based on the premise that if asked to abandon their old set of values, the nomads must be offered an alternative in the form of an insurance scheme especially created in order to protect them against emergencies which, in the past, they strove to overcome by keeping large herds.

The introduction of Livestock Development Agencies would play a crucial role in controlling nomadic activities.[14] These agencies would fulfil a three-fold role: they would act as a marketing board, as a body which would implement the national livestock policy, and as an insurance agency for the pastoral nomads.

As a marketing board they would export livestock and livestock products and they would control the prices paid to the producers. It is envisaged that the original function of accumulating reserves for the purpose of price maintenance would gradually decrease as the world prices for meat continue to rise. The accumulating financial reserves could be regarded then as a contribution to the insurance scheme against natural emergencies. They would supplement the basic insurance fund created from the stipulated proportion of the difference between the prices realized by the agency and the prices paid by it to the producers. In the initial stages foreign aid should make its contribution in order to ensure an adequate level of reserves. Part of the fund would be used for the purchase and storage of emergency stocks of fodder. The fund could also provide monies for investment and assistance loans, unless it were decided that a separate, and financially independent, credit institution should be created for the pastoral sector.

The membership of the insurance scheme would be optional but the agencies should encourage membership with all the means at their disposal.

The insurance scheme would rely on a criterion of the number of animal units calculated on a per capita basis, consistent with the maximum sustainable yield stocking density for the area as a whole. Normally the per capita quantity should not be below the number of animal units deemed necessary for human subsistence, or else reduction of the number of nomads would be required. Pastoralists who possess surplus livestock, over and above the stipulated maximum, and who regularly sell it to the agency would be offered membership of the insurance scheme. The benefits would be proportional to the amount of sales, and the latter could be encouraged by a system of premiums and fringe benefits. Nomads could be offered facilities for remunerative investment of their spare cash.

Apart from the primary purpose of providing security to the nomads the above arrangement strives to increase the off-take to the desired level. In the unlikely event of overselling, a remedy could be found in the manipulation of annually fixed purchase prices by the agency. On the other hand, nomads who refuse to sell their suplus animals would be subjected to a livestock tax imposed at rates high enough to act as a deterrent to excessive livestock accumulation. Tax rates would become progressively higher as the actual stocking density rises above the sustainable yield stocking density. Tax refunds would be made to the nomads who decide to sell the taxed animals within a prescribed period of time.[15]

Traditionally minded critics may feel apprehensive that the insurance scheme violates the sacrosanct principle of mutual help of the nomads in Africa. They may argue that such a scheme leaves out those who failed to take the necessary steps to join the scheme and find themselves now in dire need. It is possible that recipients of assistance from the insurance fund would be inclined to share it with the non-insured nomads, undermining the economic purpose of the insurance compensation. Even this difficulty can be solved. By granting credit to the destitute pastoralists the agency would help them to survive the period of hunger and permit them to restore their herds. As a condition they would be asked to join the insurance scheme and to accept its rules. Refusal to do so would result in their removal from the pastoral sector.

A final point should be made with regard to the formal aspects of the organization. Monopoly must be granted to the Livestock Development Agencies if they are to be viable. As populations are small and the per capita incomes are low, there is no room for competitors, if the economies are to benefit from the proposed insurance scheme. A single institution would be in a better position to realize economies of scale and to carry out research necessary for the most efficient administration of the scheme. It is also desirable to extend complete public control over every aspect of the agencies' important functions.

Having discussed measures for the implementation of pastoral reforms, let us now turn our attention to the relations between the pastoral sectors and the remaining sectors of the economies of which they are a part.

In the initial phase of the implementation of policies proposed in this study, the achievement of a steady state will depend on regulatory measures directed towards the establishment of a steady level of both the human and the animal populations. It can be expected that the physical output of the other sectors will grow, yet that of the pastoral sector will remain stationary, if measured over a sufficiently long period of time in order to minimize the impact of the variations in rainfall. An exception to the rigorous concept of a steady state is the possibility of improvements in the efficiency of pastoral operations. Another exception is presented by the tendency of the prices realized for livestock and livestock products to change. Their expected secular upward movement, exceeding that of other prices, would lead to improvements in the level of pastoral welfare, which is another variable permitted to change within the initial phase of the steady state. In other words, the terms of trade between the pastoral sector, other sectors of the economy and the rest of the world, would change in favour of the pastoralists.

What will happen in the following phase of development is of a highly speculative nature, unless the achievement of the limits to growth is taken as an inevitable outcome of our actions. Following this line of reasoning we must reach a conclusion that eventually a stage of zero population growth will be attained as a result of changes that are beyond the scope of our discussion. It will then not be necessary any more for the pastoral nomads to leave their sector. With the establishment of a state of global equilibrium international prices will be stabilized and so the last reason but one for changes in the level of pastoral welfare will disappear. The last source of improvement is to be found in the area of discontinuous technical progress. Thus the steady state framework will become increasingly rigid and rigorous.

Is it worth it?

From an economic point of view efforts to develop the pastoral sectors of African economies would be worthwhile if the pastoral mode of production proved a paying proposition. In terms of a private approach this means a degree of profitability which compares favourably with other avenues for investment. Nevertheless a private venture may appear profitable when some of the costs are borne by society, and are excluded from private accounts.

The fact that commercial ranchers are interested in taking over the pastoral lands points clearly to the expectations of profitability which would justify the planned investment. However, even the criterion based on their level of profitability is open to reservations. Firstly, a commercial ranch compares favourably with a pastoral family unit because, unlike the latter, it has access to modern technology and enjoys the advantages of large-scale operations. Secondly, there is no guarantee that a firm will bear all the costs of production. For these reasons one should rely primarily on a cost-benefit analysis including all the necessary inputs and outputs estimated over a period of time sufficient to take account of the returns of long-term investments in the pastoral sector. The answer thus arrived at would tell us what the development of the pastoral mode of production means for the society as a whole.

Difficulties encountered in an exercise of this kind have been already emphasized (see chapter three, section on 'Rangeland and Its Management'). Instead, the future viability of pastoralism can be assessed on the basis of the trends in variables which are important determinants of the demand for and supply of food.

Human population growth and the lagging productivity of agriculture result in a growing food deficit, which by 1985 is likely to reach between 45 and 70 million tons of foodgrains. It will represent a gap between domestic food production and the nutritional needs of the people in the less developed countries of the world.[16] FAO projections for 1970–1980[17] indicate a shortfall of meat production by 1980, amounting to 2.3 million tons. While small in relation to world production and consumption, the deficit will reach about 40 per cent of the volume of world meat trade in the base year 1970 (measured in terms of net imports). The shortfall is expected to be particularly accentuated in the production of beef and mutton. In view of the growing overall food shortage by 1985 and later, the world meat shortfall is likely to increase notwithstanding temporary and localized gluts.

The average income elasticity of demand for meat is high relative to most other foods, and with regard to beef it is higher than for any other kind of meat (0.5).[18] Earlier studies have indicated income elasticities of demand for animal proteins of 1.5 in Asia and the Far East, and 1.2 in the Middle East and Africa,[19] which are easily explicable in terms of extremely low average levels of protein consumption in those parts of the world.

In the years to come we shall have to face a rapidly growing demand for animal products, not only due to increases in per capita incomes in some of the less developed countries, but primarily as a consequence of the continuing population growth resulting in growing food grain deficits. The latter factor deserves further elaboration. Meanwhile, let us point out that the meat supply and demand situation implies rising prices particularly for beef and mutton. Given the existing price elasticities of demand this could reduce, or even eliminate, the world deficit by reducing the projected increases in the quantities demanded.[20] At the same time a faster rise in production would be encouraged. A substitution effect could also result in a change in demand patterns at the expense of the more costly protein foods.

However, there are some important reasons to believe that there are serious limitations to the extent to which production of meat can be accelerated. These are of an economic and technical nature. Let us take the United States as an example, as it is both a large producer and consumer of agricultural products. Together with Canada and Australia it is the largest grain exporter. In the U.S. an average person consumes more than 900 kilograms of grain per year, whereas in China a person is adequately fed on little more than 200 kilograms of grain per year. The difference is that on the average an American eats only 68 kilograms directly in the form of cereal or cereal products, while the balance is fed to the animals which supply him with food. The comparable quantities for a Chinese are nearly 160 and 40 kilograms respectively.[21] It is obvious that the inhabitant of the United States eats food which is much richer in animal proteins than the Chinese.

Whereas an American may consume more than 3000 calories daily, indirectly his consumption may reach about 11,000 primary calories.[22] The explanation is to be found in what the ecologists call the 'food chain'. For instance, 1000 calories that can be derived from grain suitable for human consumption, when fed to cattle, produce at most 100 to 200 calories worth of meat. Correspondingly, if one hectare of soil under cereals produces a certain number of calories, it takes between five and ten hectares to produce the same number of calories if they were to be derived from meat. For this simple reason, as the world food shortage intensifies, we shall have to feed lower on the food chains and the prices of animal protein products will tend to increase.

In 1973, U.S. farmers produced 233 million metric tons of grain of which about 44 per cent was fed to ruminants and another 21 per cent to other domestic animals.[23] Excluding wheat which is the primary cereal in the human diet, three-quarters of the other grains including corn, sorghum, barley, oats and rye were fed to livestock.[24]

Bearing in mind the projected food deficits which are more than likely to arise and to grow, as the century progresses, one is tempted to ask how many people could be fed directly with the grain at present produced in the United States and consumed by livestock alone. The figures are staggering. On varying assumptions they range between 2.8 and 5.7 billion persons annually.[25] With the use of this potential reserve the world population of the year 2000 which, on the basis of the present rate of growth, is expected to reach six billion, could still be adequately fed. In that case, of course, the inhabitants of the United States and the countries importing grain feeds from the U.S. would have to develop their own sources of forage or reduce consumption of livestock products. At present only 25 to 30 per cent of food of animal origin consumed by a typical American is based on forage.[26] Practical problems such as these, logistic aspects, and balance of payments reasons make the transfer of these formidable quantities of grain to the less developed countries highly problematical. However, it may be expected that demands will be made on the main world producers of grain to assist local efforts, in the deficit economies, to increase the supply of food grains.

A significant development took place between 1972 and 1974 in the United States when, due to the rising prices of grain, the proportion of forage in the feed of beef cattle increased from 73 to 82 per cent. At that time, forage crops supplied 63 per cent of the feed units fed to dairy cattle, and 89 per cent of those fed to sheep and goats.[27]

During the 1960s grain surpluses presented a serious problem to the North American countries. In the ensuing decade widespread crop failures in various parts of the world drew attention to the impact of the variability of climatic conditions on agriculture. In the absence of a long-term international policy aiming at the creation of buffer stocks, temporary gluts upset world market prices for grain, but it seems that it has never been fully admitted, by those who are only concerned with the current prices, that the apparently large surpluses are merely a necessary precaution. It must be considered imprudent, even for such an agriculturally strong country as the United States, to rely on one year's crop. Still in the mid-1960s an expert opinion was expressed that in the event of a serious crop failure no part of the world was more than one year away from starvation, and even the United States with all its surpluses was not more than two years away.[28]

It can be presumed that in view of the expected general trend of rising grain prices, as the world demand for grain grows, the dependence of livestock on forage crops will increase. Forage resources, so far unutilized, will have to be used more efficiently. In the United States forage crops (grasses and legumes) take up some five times the area under all grain crops, and moreover much of the land on which forages are grown is not suitable for other crops.[29]

On the world scale, of the estimated 13 billion hectares of the earth's ice-free land surface only about 3.2 billion hectares can be cultivated, but an additional 3.6 billion hectares could serve for grazing livestock, with an annual output of between 25 and 50 million live-weight metric tons which, on the average, could add a few grams of animal protein per person per day for the world population at the end of our century.[30] This would be no mean achievement as in 1965 the estimated per capita consumption of protein in North America was 94.0 grams per day, while in Africa it was only 58.2 grams. In terms of a projection made by FAO, by 1980 the African level would reach only 61.9 grams, implying a 0.4 per cent rate of growth per annum between 1965 and 1980.[31]

In addition to the importance of the protein content in food, the calorie value derived mainly from grain must also be stressed. The ruminants which are not kept on pastures are fattened for slaughter in feedlots where their movements are reduced to a minimum, as natural grazing slows their weight-gains. The same procedure is applied to hogs. These animals by consuming prodigious quantities of feed grains compete with the people in the less developed parts of the world for the scarce food supply. Moreover, they create pollution of serious dimensions through unmanageable effluent concentrations. It has been reported that in the state of Kansas alone, to take another example from the U.S., in the two hundred feedlots located there, some 5.5 million cattle and 1.3 million hogs excrete sewage equivalent to that produced by 70 million people. The nutrients present in the effluents never return to the croplands, which droppings from grazing animals used to replenish.[32] Rising costs of energy are reflected in the prices of synthetic fertilizers and fuels needed to run agricultural machinery, hence livestock fed with grain or harvested forage is increasingly costly to raise. Although much forage is grazed in the U.S. livestock industry, large amounts of it are harvested and processed before being fed to animals.[33]

Ruminants can digest forage crops which contain a relatively large proportion of cellulose, the world's most abundant organic compound.[34] Other domestic animals must rely on other foods. To maintain increasing proportions of ruminants on pasture would mean a considerable saving of non-renewable sources of energy, as the animals do the harvesting themselves and fertilize the grasslands. It would also mean an increased use of energy measured by the total digestible nutrients requirement, necessitated by the movements of the grazing animals. However, forage is a renewable source of energy. The amount of the energy-consuming movement can be reduced if proper care is taken of the quality of pastures. The experience of farmers in the more developed countries shows that very high yields of feed can be obtained from pasture if appropriate forages are grown and sound management practices are employed. In warm and moderate climates herds of cattle and sheep can be maintained on pasture except in severe winter conditions, while adequate gains of weight and a reasonably good output of milk are obtainable.[35] Compared to the reliance on grain feeds and the feedlot system with its economies of scale, natural grazing offers an increasingly competitive method of production. It is not surprising, therefore, that farmers who are slow in adjusting to the changing conditions begin to complain of competition on the part of the largely pastoral livestock raisers of South America and Oceania.

A shift towards a more widespread future use of pastures is inevitable and it will be further stimulated by the growing need for agricultural land to produce cereals for direct human consumption. More extensive use is also likely to be made of inferior pastures not suitable for the economic production of cattle and sheep. An example of a new use found for such marginal lands is an attempt to farm the red deer in Scotland, where over five million hectares of mountain, hill, moor and deer forest are available. Improvements in efficiency of production can be gained with partial domestication. Initial investigations have revealed that because of the deer's more efficient land use, the economic return should be larger than with sheep farming.[36] Experiments of this kind can open new vistas for the meat industry in a world of expanding population and shrinking natural resources. Their final success will depend on the development of the domestic and international markets for venison. The supply aspect should not present any major difficulties as the lands suitable for wildlife farming are plentiful on both sides of the Atlantic and in the Tropics, while the existing potential has hardly been touched.

Conclusions

The analysis of the pastoral sectors of several sub-Saharan economies, included in our study, reveals that the pastoral mode of production in the rain-deficient areas is, from an environmental point of view, extremely vulnerable. Because of the simple methods of production and the very limited range of natural resources pastoralism stands out as a prototype of a system in which the 'tragedy of the commons' is a normal occurrence. The distinguishing features of this microcosm and its acute problems can serve as a warning to those who live elsewhere in systems of far greater complexity.

We have found that the survival of a pastoral sector and the full realization of its potentialities require the establishment and maintenance of a steady state, and we have considered the possibilities of its various aspects and the significance of its relations with the outside world.

A pastoral reform has also been outlined without which the survival of nomadic pastoralism is highly doubtful. Unlike other proposals dealing with this problem, this stresses the element of protection against natural calamities, and a viable insurance scheme is suggested to serve as a substitute for the traditional and harmful method based on unrestrained accumulation of livestock.

Considerable space was devoted to the fundamental dilemma: whether the pastoral mode of production should be permitted to continue, or whether to turn the nomads into sedentary farmers and town-dwellers.

Having weighed the pros and cons let us return to the crucial question: is it rational to say that pastoralism is out-dated and uneconomic, and that the natural ranges should be abandoned? Such a conclusion could only be reached by those who are guided by short-term considerations and are influenced by fractional interests rather than the good of the society as a whole. The answer we have found avoids the extremes. What is required is neither the maintainance, nor a complete liquidation, of the *status quo* in the pastoral sector, but its modification.

The economic viability of pastoralism has been viewed from a general point of view, and there is little doubt that it is, and will be, the least expensive method of livestock raising. The measures suggested in this study to improve the efficiency of pastoral sectors are expected to result in considerable net gains, making pastoralism even more remunerative an occupation than it has been thus far.

African pastoral lands and the pastoralists using them are no exception, and their abandonment and elimination from the economic life of the countries of which they form an integral part would be an unforgivable mistake. The burdens involved in the resettlement of pastoral nomads would add tremendously to the problems of those least developed sub-Saharan nations, whereas the modernization of pastoral sectors would permit them to take advantage of the available developmental potential, for their own benefit and that of the rest of the world.

The vacuum created by the untimely disappearance of the nomads would attract foreign investors lured by the prospects of lucrative future gains. The enormous injustice towards the local herders could never be explained away by such concepts as the need for the superior economic efficiency of the new users of pastoral lands, or elusive benefits accruing from the employment opportunities offered to people purposely reduced to a state of destitution.

Human rights, if they are not to remain an empty word, must be linked to human values and these cannot be of an economic nature alone. Their ultimate determination is a matter of moral judgement.

NOTES

1. B. W. Hodder, 'A note on not perpetuating the status quo'. *African Affairs*, vol. 73, 1974; 159–61.
2. *Ibid.*
3. *Ibid.*
4. U.S. Department of State Statement of March 25, 29, 1977. Washington, D.C., Bureau of Public Affairs, Office of Media Services; 4 p. This statement further indicates that the expected flow of international resources to the Sahel will reach approximately one billion dollars a year by 1980. The proposed U.S. contribution will range between $100 and $150 million. It should be borne in mind that, by 1974, the emergency relief in the Sahel approached a value of US$200 million (*Africa Research Bulletin*, 1977; 4222A).
5. C. Meillassoux, 'Development or Exploitation: is the Sahel famine good business?' *Review of African Political Economy*, vol. 1, 1974; 32–3.
6. B. Kumm, 'The rains came but nomad life may be doomed', *Globe and Mail* (Toronto), 20th December, 1974; 7.
7. Z. A. Konczacki, 'Infant Malnutrition in Sub-Saharan Africa: a Problem in Socio-Economic Development', *Canadian Journal of African Studies*, vol. 6, 1972; 442.
8. G. Borgstrom, 'Ecological Aspects of Protein Feeding – The Case of Peru' in *The Careless Technology* edited by M. T. Farvar and J. P. Milton, London: Tom Stacey Ltd., 1973; 753–74.
9. C. R. Taylor, 'Ranching Arid Lands: Physiology of Wild and Domestic Ungulates in the Desert', *Botswana Notes and Records*, Special Edition no. 1, 1971; 173–5.

10. D. J. Stenning, *Savannah Nomads*. Oxford University Press, 1959; Chapter 7. I. Cunnison, 'The Social Role of Cattle', *The Sudan Journal of Veterinary Science and Animal Husbandry*, vol. 1, 1960; 8–25.
11. D. J. Stenning, *op. cit.*; 237–8.
12. *Ibid.*, 239.
13. *Ibid.*, 240.
14. The name is identical with that of an institution existing in Somalia, but its functions would be considerably extended.
15. The issue of cattle-tax remittance is discussed by D. J. Stenning with reference to the pastoral Fulani (*op. cit.*; 246). He points out that measures of this nature ignore the basic ecological conditions in which herd husbandry is carried out. Until these conditions are modified no significant part of a herd will be regarded by its pastoral owners as surplus. In our case, however, the impact of the ecological conditions is lessened by the insurance scheme.
16. S. J. Burki and T. J. Goering, 'Food problems of the low-income countries', *Finance and Development*, vol. 14, 1977; 15.
17. FAO., Agricultural Commodity Projections, 1970–1980, CCP 71/20 Rome 1971, vol. 1; 134–5.
18. *Ibid.*, 127.
19. FAO., Agricultural Commodity Projections for 1970, vol. 1; 25.
20. *Ibid.*, 135.
21. J. Mayer, 'The Dimensions of Human Hunger', *Scientific American*, vol. 325, 1976; 47.
22. G. Borgstrom, *The Hungry Planet*. New York: Collier Books, 1967; 28–9.
23. H. J. Hodgson, 'Forage Crops', *Scientific American*, vol. 234, 1976; 68–9.
24. *Ibid.*
25. The figure of 2.8 billion is based on the assumption of 44 per cent of the U.S. output of grains in 1973, and a daily diet of 1 kilogram of grain per day per person, which provides for the minimum protein requirement from corn (the principal feed grain). The figure of 5.7 billion persons is based on the assumption of 65 per cent of the U.S. output of grains in 1973, and a daily diet of 0.7 kilogram, providing for 2600 calories per day. The latter norm is an average intake of 3000 calories per day for a man, and 2200 calories for a woman, defined by the U.N. as adequate. The above estimate tends to be conservative as it assumes that every person is an adult.
26. H. J. Hodgson, *loc. cit.*; 74.
27. *Ibid.*, 68.
28. G. Borgstrom, *op. cit.*; 349–50.
29. H. J. Hodgson, *loc. cit.*; 60.
30. R. Revelle, 'The Resources Available for Agriculture', *Scientific American*, vol. 235, 1976; 174–7.
31. E. A. Okwuosa, *New Direction for Economic Development in Africa*, London: Africa Books, 1976; 127.
32. G. Garvey, *Energy, Ecology, Economy*. New York: W. W. Norton & Co. 1972; 65–7.
33. H. J. Hodgson, *loc. cit.*; 60.

34. *Ibid.*, 74.
35. *Ibid.*, 67.
36. M. de Meuron-Landolt, 'Farming the red deer', *New Scientist*, 5 June, 1975; 545–8.

APPENDIX A

Protection of Indigenous and Tribal Populations

General human rights, referred to at the end of chapter seven, have been officially stated on several occasions. A formal statement of these rights, particularly appropriate to the case of African pastoralists, can be found in the text of a Convention adopted at the general conference of the International Labour Organization, on the 26th June, 1957, and referred to as the Indigenous and Tribal Populations Convention of 1957.*

A summary is given below of the provisions of this Convention which are essential in the context of our proposed pastoral reform.

The basic statement of human rights from which the provisions of the Convention follow is the affirmation in the Declaration of Philadelphia '... that all human beings have the right to pursue both their material wellbeing and their spiritual development in conditions of freedom and dignity, of economic security and equal opportunity ...'

As a matter of general policy governments are responsible for developing co-ordinated and systematic action for the protection of the populations concerned and their progressive integration into the life of their respective countries. But measures leading towards the artificial assimilation of these populations and recourse to force or coercion shall be excluded (Article 2). The danger involved in disrupting the values and institutions of the populations concerned unless they can be replaced by appropriate and acceptable substitutes shall be recognized, and policies aimed at mitigating the difficulties experienced by these populations in adjusting themselves to new conditions of life and work shall be adopted (Article 4).

* Its full title is: 'Convention concerning the protection and integration of indigenous and other tribal and semi-tribal populations in independent countries' (Convention 107).

In applying the provisions of the Convention governments shall seek the collaboration of these populations and of their representatives and provide them with opportunities for the full development of their initiative (Article 5).

Improvements in conditions of life and work and level of education will be assisted by specially designed projects for economic development of the areas in question (Article 6).

With regard to land, Article 11 of the Convention stipulates that the right of ownership, collective or individual, of the members of the populations concerned, over the lands which these populations traditionally occupy shall be recognized. Furthermore, the populations shall not be removed, without their free consent, from their habitual territories except in accordance with national laws and regulations for reasons relating to national security, or in the interest of national economic development or of the health of the said populations. In the case of removal they shall be provided with lands of quality at least equal to that of the lands previously occupied by them. In cases where chances of alternative employment exist and where the populations concerned prefer to have compensation in money or in kind, they shall be so compensated under appropriate guarantees (Article 12).

Procedures for the transmission of rights of ownership and use of land which are established by the customs of the populations concerned shall be respected. Arrangements shall be also made to prevent persons who are not members of the populations concerned from taking advantage of these customs or of lack of understanding of the laws on the part of the members of these populations to secure the ownership or use of the lands belonging to such members (Article 13).

The Convention becomes binding only upon those Members of the International Labour Organization who have ratified it, and comes into force for any Member twelve months after the date on which its ratification has been registered (Article 31).

APPENDIX B

Conversion Table

Metric unit	Abbreviation	Equivalent
kilometre	km	0.62 mile
metre	m	39.37 inches
centimetre	cm	0.39 inch
millimetre	mm	0.04 inch
square kilometre	sq. km or km²	0.3861 square mile
hectare	ha	2.47 acres
metric ton	MT or t	1.1 tons
quintal	q	220.46 pounds
kilogram	kg	2.2046 pounds
gram	g or gm	0.035 ounce

APPENDIX C

A Postscript: Recent Plans for Arid and Semi-arid Zones

Since the completion of the manuscript some new events have occurred which deserve to be noted: firstly the launching of a long-term economic plan for the recovery of the Sahel; secondly, the U.N. Conference on Desertification; and thirdly, the publication of a new Botswana National Development Plan 1976–81.

The plan for the Sahel region was published early in 1977, as a report of the Organization for Economic Co-operation and Development, and was approved at a meeting of the Club of Friends of the Sahel, which was held at Ottawa (Canada) in June of that year. The Plan is to cost $10,000 million, and is to be implemented over a 20-year period. The first phase, ending in 1982, will involve an expenditure of $3,000 million.[1]

The United Nations Conference on Desertification (UNCOD) took place in Nairobi (Kenya) between 29th August and 9th September 1977. It was organized under the auspices of the U.N. Environment Programme, and was attended by more than 2,000 delegates from 110 countries.

The drafting of a plan of action was the main concern of the Conference. Priority was accorded to the creation of green belts along the fringes of the Sahara, management of livestock and rangelands, and monitoring desertification processes in the arid and semi-arid areas of the world.

At present, desertification, in various parts of the world, threatens the livelihood of at least 60 million people. Eventually it may affect approximately 14 per cent of the world's population living in the drylands.[2]

Botswana's National Development Plan 1976–81 replaces the previous Plan, which was to cover the period 1973–78.[3] Like its predecessor it is a rolling plan and is subject to a revision every three years.

Development expenditure guidelines indicate an expenditure of P250 million (at 1976–77 prices) on the total core development programme.[4] An additional amount of P25 million is allowed for the 'interplan' projects which are expected to arise in the later years of the planning period.

Seventy-nine million Pula of the proposed development expenditure are expected to be financed out of local sources. Foreign aid funds already approved, or under negotiation, will provide P151 million, and the balance of P45 million remains to be negotiated.

The Government's main objectives remain largely the same as those outlined in the 1973–78 Plan. The planners have assumed that the mineral and livestock sectors are the most dynamic elements in Botswana's development and a recent economic forecast indicates that this trend will continue, even if the growth of both these sectors is less dramatic than in the past. The new Plan stresses the need for expansion of other sectors as well, including non-livestock agriculture, industry, and commerce, as their growth is of direct benefit to a large proportion of the population.

The Programme favours urban areas and as much as 36 per cent of total expenditure will be earmarked for their development, compared to 29 per cent allocated to rural areas. Communication projects account for 32 per cent of planned expenditure. The preponderance of communications and other infrastructural projects reflects the importance attached to the provision of basic infrastructure and the high cost of construction in a large and thinly populated country. By contrast expenditure on agriculture of P24.1 million, or barely 9 per cent of the total, appears to be relatively low, when it is remembered that 85 per cent of the population is rural. The dominant position of livestock in Botswana's economy is reflected in the proportion of resources allocated to livestock development amounting to P17.7 million, or 73.4 per cent of expenditure on agriculture. It is to be understood, however, that many infrastructural projects are designed to help rural people in general, and livestock owners in particular.

By far the most important innovation is the incorporation in the Plan of the Tribal Grazing Land Programme (TGLP), based on the Government Paper No. 2 of 1975 (see pp. 143–147 above). The tenure reforms of the TGLP represent the first stage of a nation-wide effort to conserve Botswana's livestock resources. To be fully effective these reforms will have to be accompanied by improved management practices if the degradation of the grazing lands is to be halted and reversed. The Plan introduces a Range and Livestock Management

Project, the purpose of which is to investigate such forms of group ranches as are both economically and socially acceptable to the smaller farmers. Also, Service Companies will be formed to cater to the needs of ranches which require services that no single ranch unit can afford. Apart from advice, the Companies will provide for borehole maintenance, firebreak construction, bulk purchase of inputs, and marketing arrangements.

Increased livestock production and control over the size of animal population are to be achieved by increasing the off-take. During the early 1970's annual off-take from the national herd averaged 9.6 per cent. It is planned to increase annual off-take to 13 per cent by 1990. The proposed reform of the ranching system will help to achieve this goal, provided additional marketing facilities are created. The extension of abattoir capacity is considered to be a prerequisite in the expansion of cattle production. The present daily throughput capacity of 1,200 head is unable to cope with the off-take requirements of a national herd which already in 1976 reached an estimated three million head. The situation would become critical in the event of a drought.

The positive aspect of the Plan lies in the fact that it relies, to a much greater extent than its predecessor, on medium- and long-term projections.

Attention is paid to the rapid population growth and to the demands it will create if an acceptable living standard is to be attained by all citizens. The 1991 projection in the present Plan assumes that there is no permanent emigration, that fertility remains constant and that mortality continues to decline. An average annual population growth rate of 3.3 per cent, obtained on the basis of these assumptions, suggests that by 1991 Botswana's economy will have to support 557,000 more people than in 1971. Furthermore, it is assumed that as a result of internal migration the urban population will increase by 1991 from the present 10 per cent to 26 per cent of total population. Despite rapid urbanization, in thirteen years' time, the rural economy will have to support more than half as many people again as it did in 1971.

Let us consider briefly the economic alternatives to meet the demands created by rapid population growth. The first approach assumes that the livestock sector remains static after a decade of steady development, while other agriculture keeps pace with the growth of rural population, and the mineral sector continues to expand at a steady, but not a spectacular rate. Under this alternative the GDP grows at an average 3.4 per cent p.a.

The second alternative is based on similar assumptions except that exploitation of coal reserves for export is developed. As a result there is a startling increase in the rate of growth of the GDP, which rises to 13.4 per cent p.a.

The third alternative postulates that a 6.0 per cent p.a. GDP growth rate could be achieved without continuing mineral windfalls, but by ensuring growth rates of 7.2 per cent in the livestock sector, and 4.0 per cent in other agriculture.

Under the first alternative per capita income would grow at about 0.1 per cent p.a., and employment would increase less than population. Under the second alternative employment would grow between two and three percentage points faster than population. The third alternative stresses the maximum expansion of arable and livestock agriculture, and has the advantage of not being entirely dependent on windfalls. Moreover, it is consistent with Government strategy, which relies largely on sectors which are more amenable to Government influence than the mineral sector.

Bearing in mind the highly speculative nature of the above alternatives it should be observed that they could be modified still further by the introduction of policies planned to reduce the pressure of population growth. The long-term projections can be also affected by disruptive contingencies such as an unfavourable shift in the terms of trade, a drought, a delay in mineral expansion, to name a few. The possibility of regional political upheavals could lead to major geopolitical changes in Southern Africa. Their potential effects could be incalculable.

NOTES

1. *Africa Research Bulletin*, May 15–June 14, 1977; 4296
2. *Ibid.*, August 15–September 14, 1977; 4390
3. Republic of Botswana, *National Development Plan 1976–81*, Gaborone, 1977.
4. On 23 August 1976, Botswana adopted a new currency, the Pula, which replaced the South African Rand. Until 1 December 1976, the Bank of Botswana was under obligation to maintain a one-to-one exchange of the Rand for the Pula, after which date the rate of exchange may be altered at Botswana's discretion.

INDEX